PRINCESS ELIZABETH

*The Illustrated Story
of Twenty-one Years
in the Life of the
Heir Presumptive*

By
DERMOT MORRAH
Late Fellow of All Souls College, Oxford
assisted by
Betty Spencer Shew

1947

ODHAMS PRESS LIMITED · LONG ACRE · LONDON

AFTER THE CORONATION—12th MAY, 1937

HEIR TO THE THRONE

JUST a century has elapsed, in this year 1947, since Alfred Tennyson published his ironic medley about the "women's movement," and called it *The Princess*. The future poet laureate would not have been a man of his age if he had not made elegant fun of the pretty creatures' absurd claim to be the equals of the lordly male. But he would not have been a devoted subject of the Sovereign Lady, who was to be so great and of whose greatness he was to be the interpreter, if he had not perceived a potentiality in womanhood to which his world gave no scope, and suspected that that which he permitted his characters to mock might be in truth the reality of the future. And so, although he leaves the issue between the mockers and the realists unsettled, Tennyson's inmost feelings seem to be with the romantics, in a vision of an equal companionship of the sexes, in which woman shall

> set herself to man,
> Like perfect music unto noble words;
> And so these twain, upon the skirts of Time,
> Sit side by side, full-summ'd in all their powers,
> Dispensing harvest, sowing the To-be.

A hundred years have resolved the poet's uncertainties, and driven the mockers in disorder from the field. Man and woman indeed "sit side by side, full-summ'd in all their powers" at every level of public life up to the very Cabinet itself. More than that, and a thing that Tennyson had not imagined even as a subject of caricature, they have stood side by side in the blue and khaki of the fighting services under fire. And a nation that has grown accustomed to these things is proud and content to see the future symbolized in the person of The Princess. Princess Elizabeth stands to the men and women of today for the hope of a world set free at last from the forces of destruction, for the spirit of all that generation, of both sexes, which will be charged tomorrow with the responsibility for an Empire's destiny, and today is endeavouring to learn, from the awful experience of all but universal catastrophe, the art that can make humanity master of its fate.

She is herself the first learner of them all, for she is apprenticed to the great craft of monarchy.

She is learning her business, that is to say, no longer as a schoolroom task or a theoretic art, but by actually assisting a master craftsman in his daily labours. The transition in Princess Elizabeth's case has been gradual; but the conspicuous place allotted to her in the royal tour of South Africa shows that by her twenty-first birthday it is complete. More and more we shall come to think of her as the articled associate of sovereignty over the whole vast range of the King's work for the Empire.

The aspect of this work that first presents itself to the mind, though under modern conditions it is scarcely the most important, is the part that the King takes in the political government of his dominions, and especially of the United Kingdom, where he normally resides. Although under the Constitution he acts exclusively on the advice of the Ministers who, for the time being, command the confidence of Parliament, he exercises a very real and profound personal influence. He shares all the secrets of the Cabinet—they are indeed technically his secrets rather than theirs; he keeps in touch with every branch of high policy. And, since Governments come and go but the King remains, he gradually acquires a continuous experience richer and more varied than any party statesman can hope to possess. He is always accessible for consultation; and although in constitutional form his Ministers advise him, there are few of them who cannot recall occasions when he has most valuably, though informally, been able to advise *them*.

Now since this personal contribution of the Sovereign to government depends mainly on the duration of his direct contact with administration, it will be of evident value if experience can begin to be acquired before accession to the throne; and in fact it has long been customary to give the heir apparent, as well as the King, access to all the most important State papers. (Queen Victoria was much criticized for excluding her eldest son from any considerable dealing with high policy until he was far advanced in middle age.) There is no precedent for giving an heiress the key to the dispatch cases in which Cabinet documents are circulated; but the position of women in public

ON BUCKINGHAM PALACE BALCONY, VE-DAY—8th MAY, 1945

life has vastly changed since last one of them was heir to the throne, and no one will be surprised if steps are taken before long to give Princess Elizabeth personal contact with the routine of government. In this way it may be expected that, by the time she becomes Queen, she will already have grasped all those threads of long-term policy which continue from Parliament to Parliament, only slightly deflected by the particular party that happens to be in power.

Secondly, the King helps government by being on terms of personal friendship with the group of men who for the time being form his administration; and this friendship will in the nature of things continue after their opponents have thrown them out of office, even though he must then cease to discuss policy with them. Thus, by being on equally good personal terms with both sides, the King can do much to smooth the intercourse of politicians, and to encourage that sense of comradeship in the adventure of public service, which unites men at a deeper level than the acrimonies of debate, and has for generations been the distinguishing mark and the pride of British Parliaments.

Here, too, the heiress has a vital part to play. She must learn to know the leaders of the nation,

whatever their party, who might some day be her Ministers; perhaps especially she should interest herself in those who have not yet come to the highest place, but are likely to be the leaders of the future. Princess Elizabeth has been accustomed to meet, as the daughter of any less exalted family would do, all those who visit her father's house, and has thus already begun to acquire that knowledge of the men of mark in the land, knowledge which she will require as Queen.

Before leaving the political functions of Princess Elizabeth as heir to the throne, it is necessary to mention certain formal duties which are laid upon her by statute. She is not only the King's associate and assistant, but in certain circumstances his appointed understudy. In the event of serious illness, which totally incapacitates him for the discharge of his royal duties, the Princess becomes Regent of the United Kingdom, enjoying nearly all the powers of the King himself. If on the other hand he is absent from the realm, the royal prerogative is to be jointly exercised by a committee of five, called Councillors of State, who are to be the Queen and the four adults of the Royal Family who are nearest to the succession. Although the Princess, like any other subject, does not come of age till she is twenty-one,

ceremonies here express real and profound feeling. In all the stately and glowing solemnities of Church and State, which are carried on in order that the people may see in the mirror of royalty some reflection of the inheritance they have received and the proud fellowship in which they share, the heiress is expected to go her processional way as a figure only less striking in its majesty than are the figures of the King and Queen themselves. There must be times when her human personality will be deliberately submerged in the pomp and circumstance of the part she plays.

She is required to be impressive when she appears as a symbolic figure on state occasions, she is equally required effectively to carry through the other and more intimate form of royal representation. In the latter role she has to sum up for her future subjects all that is most characteristic of their own lives, the normal life of normal British people, distilled as it were into its essence. She must be able to enter into the minds of all sorts and conditions of people, and they must feel that they can in some degree enter into hers; so that as she moves among them at their work and at their play it may seem that through her a message of friendship and understanding is conveyed between the whole nation, or indeed the whole Empire, and one of its parts. It may be only a very humble part, but in that moment it is given worth and dignity.

This is a kingly function, and in a larger sense a function shared by all the Royal Family. The Princess, as in all else that belongs to her station, will be preparing herself to discharge it in its primary form by making herself ultimately the true representative of the whole Empire, distributed about the world, and of the unbroken tradition of its past, its present, and its future. In concrete terms, she must travel widely in space, in order to make personal contact with all its peoples; she must travel in time, by making herself acquainted with its history. That is the preparatory side of her mission as representative. But it has a more immediate and active side. Although she is to become eventually the supreme representative of the whole, it is natural at this stage of her career that she should be in a special sense the representative of a part. She should stand particularly for the young, becoming at once the leader of the generation which has

a special amendment to the Regency Act was passed, which qualified her for the position of Councillor of State from the age of eighteen; and in fact she was more than once a Councillor of State during the King's visits to his troops abroad during the war, although, for security reasons, no publicity could be given to the appointment. If the Queen is absent with the King, the Princess becomes the head of the Council.

But, as has been said, it is not in the domain of politics that modern royalty plays its most characteristic part. The King is above all the supreme representative, uniting all the threads of the Empire's life in his own person, helping its many communities scattered round the globe to feel that they are one family of which he is the head, linking the traditions of the past to the hopes of the future by his embodiment of both in the present. This supremely important function of kingship and queenship Princess Elizabeth has to prepare herself to take up, and that mainly by sharing in its exercise.

Now there are two aspects of the royal representation. There is first the ceremonial side. Many foreign observers have remarked that the British have a genius for pageantry that no other nation approaches; and if this is true, it is because

VICTORY TOUR OF EAST END OF LONDON—9th MAY, 1945

reached maturity with her; she will represent indeed the undying spirit of Britain, but with all the emphasis upon the future, upon what it is becoming more than what it has been.

In her public capacity she will naturally give her patronage to the many organizations seeking to advance the interests of young people: she will gather about her young men and women who may be expected to influence the fortunes of the people in the coming years. When she has a home of her own, it may be expected to become a centre of hospitality where new ideas, hopeful but not yet sufficiently proven to call for the recognition of the Sovereign in person, may be discussed and encouraged. This has always been in some sense customary with heirs to the throne, although in the past it has taken a different shape from any now conceivable for, in the Hanoverian reigns when the King exercised his personal influence in favour of one of the political parties, the house of the Prince of Wales was apt to be the centre of intrigue for the groups in opposition who hoped to be swept to power when the new reign should begin. There is now no danger that such a disastrous rivalry will recur; first, because the King's Court is nowadays no longer a headquarters of party politics and, secondly, because the unhappy tradition of family feuds which darkened the records of the Hanoverian dynasty has given place to an ideal relationship, in which mutual confidence between father and daughter is self-evident to the world.

And in this connection one other thing should be said. The Princess is the natural representative of the generation into which she is born, that of the young men and women who have grown up as their country moves out of the shadows of the Second World War. She does not represent them only as workers, or as voters, or predominantly in their more serious moods. She stands for their whole life, and more especially, if anything, on its lighter side. For youth is a time for enjoyment; and for the youth of this generation above all, whose childhood has been overshadowed by the privations, the dangers, and the sheer tedium of war, it needs to be asserted publicly that they have a right to a full share of amusement and carefree happiness. This is perhaps what Goethe meant when he said that youth itself was the education of the young. The proper person to assert their rights in this regard is their chief, the King's young daughter. They have their work to do and so has she; they will see her performing a strenuous round, and hear her voice uplifted upon occasions. But they will also see her dancing and riding and sailing, and dining out, watching football matches and race meetings (and from time to time backing her fancy like any other enthusiast); in fact, giving rein to native high spirits in the sort of gaiety that the world owes to any girl of her years, and of late has generally denied. When she is thus enjoying herself she is playing as royal and as valuable a part as if she were driving, robed and coroneted, in some State procession; for she is preaching by practice the wholesome doctrine that the millions of young men and women of the post-war Commonwealth, who are born to share her birthright and are at heart very like her, are entitled to the guerdon of youth and will be better citizens for it. The photographs of the Princess, which illustrate this volume, show her nearly always in happy moods; and naturally, because her happy moments are many, and it is for happiness above all that she stands and should stand in the national life.

It is a curious historical fact that no Queen of England has in the course of nature succeeded to her father; and no reigning sovereign until King George VI has brought up his daughter as his successor. To this generalization there are certain apparent exceptions. Although Queen Victoria was the niece of her two predecessors, George IV and William IV, all our other queens regnant were the daughters of kings. But Henry VIII, the father of Mary I and Elizabeth, was immediately succeeded by his son, their younger brother Edward VI; and James II, the father of Mary II and Anne, did not in the ordinary course of nature vacate the throne that the elder of them ascended, but was deposed by a successful revolution, which set her, jointly with her husband, William III, in his place. Moreover, Mary was in no sense his heiress, for he had a son, afterwards known to the Jacobites as James III (of England) and VIII (of Scotland) and to the Whigs as the Old Pretender; she and William reigned by no hereditary right, but by a purely parliamentary title.

It is further true that two princesses, far separated by the centuries, have been designated by their fathers as their successors. At a great council in London early in the year 1127, King Henry I, who had lost his only son in the tragic wreck of the *White Ship*, caused the magnates of the realm to swear allegiance to his daughter Maud as their future queen. But she was then twenty-four and already the widow of a foreign monarch, the Emperor Henry V; and since within a few months she was sent abroad again as the bride of Geoffrey Plantagenet, Count of Anjou, it clearly cannot be considered that King Henry in any sense brought her up for the position he designed for her. She figures in our history as the Empress Maud (or Matilda), who fought King Stephen through some of the most miserable years of our history, and eventually as the mother of the great King Henry II; but she was never crowned and is not reckoned among the queens regnant of England.

Nearly seven centuries after the Empress Maud, a daughter, the Princess Charlotte, was born in 1796 to George, Prince of Wales, afterwards George IV, and his wife Caroline of Brunswick. Since her parents, in a clearly irreconcilable quarrel, separated soon afterwards, it became evident very early in her life that she was unlikely ever to have a brother; and she was universally recognized as destined to be Queen of England. It stands to the credit of the Prince Regent, in whose private character history has not found much to praise, that, scrupulously shielding his daughter from all contact with the dissipated life he led, he caused her to be brought up under a careful discipline especially devised to prepare her for her exalted destiny. As she came to womanhood Princess Charlotte gathered to herself a widespread popularity, becoming indeed the very embodiment of the whole people's aspirations for the future. But, having been married to Prince Leopold of Saxe-Coburg, afterwards the first King of the Belgians, she died in giving birth to a stillborn child. She was only twenty-one; and she did not live to see her father King.

This pathetic figure, whose short life ended almost where that of Princess Elizabeth may be said to begin, affords the nearest parallel in history to the position occupied by the present heiress. One outstanding contrast, however, has to be noted. The national affection that was poured out upon Princess Charlotte was rooted in the hope that her accession would be the signal for the reversal of everything in public policy, and especially in the life of the Court, for which her father had stood. Precisely the opposite is true of Princess Elizabeth. She inherits her share in the personal devotion that her parents have won, by their own record of selfless service, in the hearts of all their subjects; and the enthusiasm that greets her coming of age expresses the national feeling that, when her time comes, she will continue to lead them in the paths that King George and Queen Elizabeth have marked out.

Of the previous queens regnant of England, only the blood of Queen Victoria, her great-

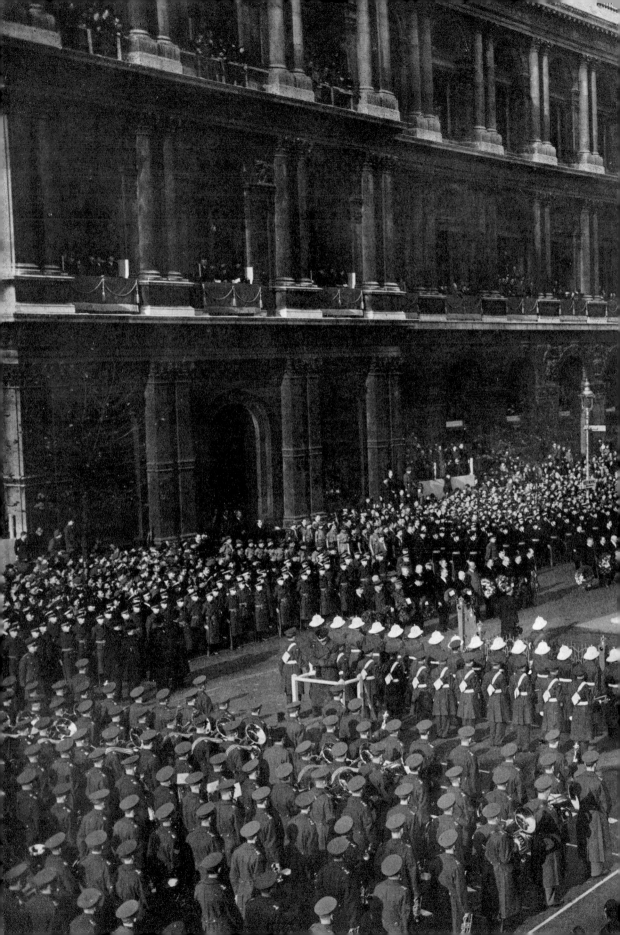

REMEMBRANCE DAY—10th NOVEMBER, 1946

great-grandmother, flows in the Princess's veins; indeed no other queen left descendants. But the United Kingdom to which she is heir was formed by the union of two equal partners; and among her ancestresses she counts the most famous of all the sovereigns of Scotland. As King James V lay dying in despair at Falkland, after the great defeat at the Battle of Solway Moss, word was brought to him that the Queen had given birth at Linlithgow to "ane fair dochter." But he "turned his back to the lords and his face to the wall," muttering: "It came with a lass an' it will gang with a lass." He was referring to the way that the Stewarts two centuries before had reached the throne, by marriage with Marjorie, daughter and eventual heiress of King Robert the Bruce; and now he seemed to foresee their loss of it, when his own daughter should carry the inheritance into a new family. As it happened, he was a bad prophet; for Mary Queen of Scots married another Stewart, her cousin Lord Darnley, and their son doubled the glory of the family by inheriting England as well as Scotland. History in that respect is not likely to repeat itself; but an age less preoccupied with purely dynastic considerations will not be unduly perturbed by the prospect that the British Crown will naturally pass, with Princess Elizabeth's descendants, out of the male line of Saxe-Coburg-Gotha, greatly as that family has made itself respected and beloved.

But although it is true that this queen of romance was the daughter and successor of a king, it is difficult to see in her a forerunner of Princess Elizabeth; for she became Queen of Scots at the age of one week, and had little opportunity to explore the problems that beset the heiress to a throne.

The upshot, then, of this brief review of previous heiresses to the English, Scottish, and British crowns is that the position of Princess Elizabeth is unique in history. She has no predecessor of her own sex whom she can make her model—not, for instance, Queen Victoria, who was kept in strict seclusion until she was eighteen and then at once became Queen. Born as she is to that inward loneliness which is in the nature of things the lot of royalty, she has a peculiar loneliness of her own, deriving from her special relationship to the historic tradition in which she stands. Stepping out therefore, on her twenty-first birthday, along a path of public service that no one has trodden quite in the same way before, Her Royal Highness has a right to something more than loyalty; she needs the personal sympathy of all those who will one day be her subjects. The task that awaits her in life is as exacting as can confront any human being; she can only discharge it with the constant goodwill and support of all the peoples in whose cause it is undertaken.

A moment may be spared here to explain the legal provisions that place Princess Elizabeth in the position of what is called "heir presumptive." The Crown of Great Britain is held under the Act of Settlement, 1701, which was passed at the end of the reign of William III to provide for the succession in case both he and the next heiress, Princess Anne, should die—as actually happened—without surviving issue. Determined as the two Houses of Parliament were to continue the exclusion of Anne's Catholic brother, they named as next heir after her the Electress Sophia of Hanover, the Protestant granddaughter of James I and sister of the Cavalier leader, Prince Rupert; Sophia in her turn was to be succeeded by her "heirs general" for ever, provided that they also were Protestants. This remarkable old lady incidentally, presents, perhaps, the greatest contrast to Princess Elizabeth in the list of heiresses to the British throne. She never saw England or learned its language. She became heiress at seventy-two and is thought to have kept herself alive till the age of eighty-four by sheer determination to outlive Queen Anne and enjoy her long-postponed inheritance. She failed by two months, and her son succeeded as George I. Yet every sovereign who has reigned over us since 1714 has held his throne as heir general of this half forgotten German princess.

Now in our common and statute law the expression "heir general" means in the first place the eldest son of the eldest male line—all the brothers in turn being entitled to succeed in preference to any of the sisters. But if a holder of the inheritance dies leaving no son (or descendant of a son), his daughters and their children will come in before his younger brothers. Thus Queen Victoria succeeded and not her uncle Ernest, who was younger than her father, Edward, Duke of Kent. It is true that the ordinary law does not give preference to an elder over a younger sister, as it does with brothers; real property is divided

INSPECTING THE GRENADIER GUARDS—MAY, 1945

equally between them and a peerage inheritable by heirs general goes into abeyance. But such a rule cannot tolerably be applied to the Crown, which of its nature is incapable of being divided or held in suspense. The case of two "co-heiresses general" has never arisen since the Act of Settlement. But the succession of John Baliol to the throne of Scotland in 1292, as descendant of the eldest niece of King William the Lion, and James I to England in 1603, as a descendant of the elder daughter of Henry VII, constitutes partial precedents; and no doubt these were in the mind of the Attorney General when he told Parliament in 1937, though he did not give his reasons, that there was no doubt about the legal right of the elder daughter of King George VI to be regarded as sole heir presumptive to the throne.

This does not, however, place her in quite the same position as would be occupied by a male heir. The eldest son of a king is described in his father's lifetime as "heir apparent," that is, the visible heir, because nothing but death can prevent his ultimately becoming entitled to the inheritance. Any more indirect heir—for instance the brother or daughter of a king who has no son—can only be "heir presumptive," because he or she only succeeds *presuming* that no heir apparent is born. There is only one way in which a woman can be heir apparent—that is when she is the daughter of a sovereign's eldest son who has died before his father; but this case has never occurred in British history.

Princess Elizabeth, then, is heir presumptive, not heir apparent. Although the British peoples have long since come to regard her eventual succession as practically certain, we must not be misled into thinking that the distinction between the two kinds of heir is a lawyers' fiction, and not a real difference. The future Queen Mary II, for instance, remained heir presumptive until the age of twenty-six, when her half-brother James was born; and in fact, as has been said, it was the Revolution of 1688, and not the course of natural succession, that brought her the Crown. Queen

COMPETING AT WINDSOR HORSE SHOW—MAY, 1945

Mary I was heir presumptive to Henry VIII for twenty-one years; then came the heir apparent in the person of the future Edward VI. The circumstances in both cases were quite unlike those which prevail today; but law and custom have to provide rules that will meet all circumstances.

These legal technicalities and historical instances have been introduced here for a purpose. It is sometimes asked—particularly and very understandably by patriotic Welshmen—whether Princess Elizabeth will shortly be created Princess of Wales. The answer is implicit in the distinction between an heir apparent and an heir presumptive. By continuous tradition since the reign of Edward III, the dignity of Prince of Wales has been conferred upon every heir apparent, and upon no other person whatsoever. Twice it has been given to a king's grandson who became heir apparent by the death of his father—the future Richard II and George III. But it has never been given to an heir presumptive, male or female—neither to those who eventually succeeded their brothers as James II and William IV, nor to any of the five princesses who became reigning queens. It is sometimes said that Henry VIII made his daughter Mary, Princess of Wales; and he did indeed send her to keep her court at Ludlow as nominal head of the government of the principality, where she was commonly given the title by courtesy. But no letters patent conferring the dignity have ever been discovered, nor can any have existed, for if they had they would have prevented the bestowal of it later upon her brother Edward.

Now there is no formal law governing these things, and it is within the King's power to break away from the past and for the first time make the heiress presumptive Princess of Wales. As has been said, Princess Elizabeth's position is unique in history, and many unprecedented things have been and will be done by her and for her. But all the value and the romance of this great dignity reside in its history, its traditions, and the immemorial customs that govern its bestowal. If a departure from custom were now made, even to meet the exceptional case of a king's daughter who is being brought up, more deliberately than any of her ancestresses, as her father's destined successor, a new precedent would be created and the old customs proportionately weakened. The Principality of Wales would descend to after ages as something different from that which we have

known; future heirs or heiresses presumptive might be held to have a moral claim to it; and sooner or later some king's son, born perhaps in like circumstances to the child of 1688, would find that his birthright had been given to another before he was born.

There are certain other dignities normally belonging to the heir apparent, of which the most important are the Dukedom of Cornwall and the Earldom of Chester. The Dukedom, the first example of that rank to be created in England, was bestowed by charter upon the Black Prince in 1339; and the charter is still in force. By its terms the duchy goes automatically to the King's eldest son, and can belong to no other person; even the future kings Richard II and George III, though they were made Princes of Wales on the deaths of their respective fathers, could not be Dukes of Cornwall. A Duchess of Cornwall in her own right is a legal impossibility.

The Earldom of Chester is not quite in the same case. It does not, like the Dukedom of Cornwall, belong automatically to the heir apparent, but is freshly created in each reign. But its creation is subject to certain customary rules, the purpose of which is to keep it available for future heirs. Being a peerage, it is of its nature hereditary; though this characteristic is veiled, since it repeatedly merges in the Crown on the accession of the Earl. But if a woman, though heir presumptive, were made Countess of Chester, and then an heir apparent were born, she might marry and have children, and thus carry the earldom by inheritance away from the royal house. The rule of custom has therefore ordained that only the King's son or grandson shall be made Earl of Chester.

There are of course other royal dignities with ancient and romantic associations to which these objections do not apply. When a dukedom is bestowed upon a king's younger son, it is always with a provision that it shall pass after him to his male heirs; and thus the probability that it will become in the course of generations entirely detached from the Royal Family is fully accepted. From this point of view the position of a daughter does not differ from that of a younger son. If, therefore, the King should wish to give his heiress high rank in the peerage, the several dukedoms established by custom as royal, so far as they are at present vacant, are all at his disposal. It has not indeed been done before. Queen Victoria was never a peeress, partly no doubt because she was barely eighteen when she ascended the throne. Before her time the accepted way of giving rank to a woman was through her husband. Prince Leopold, it is said, was just about to be made Duke of Kendal when his wife, Princess Charlotte, came to her untimely death; Queen Anne, before her accession, had become a duchess through the bestowal of the Dukedom of Cumberland on her husband, Prince George of Denmark. Her elder sister, Mary II, needed no English ennoblement, having married the Prince of Orange long before her father came to the throne. As for the two queenly daughters of Henry VIII, though they were in turn regarded as unsatisfactory makeshift heirs until the birth of his son, for most of their father's reign they were sufficiently pleased to keep their heads on their shoulders, without troubling overmuch about a coronet to adorn them.

There are, therefore, no very firm precedents to influence the King's free decision on this question. There is an evident advantage of simplicity in waiting until the Princess's marriage and then conferring on her husband any dignity it is desired she should enjoy; for thus it would be shared between them, as would not be the case if it were bestowed upon her separately. But there is one constitutional possibility to be taken into account. By immemorial tradition the King's heir—normally as Duke of Cornwall—has ranked as the head of the Second Estate of the Realm, the Lords Temporal in the Upper House of Parliament. At present the House of Lords does not acknowledge any right of women to be summoned to its counsels. But very few male strongholds nowadays are able to hold out indefinitely against the assaults of the other sex; and it would be rash to consider it impossible that, in the course of the present reign, either a new statute or a reinterpretation of the existing law may bring into being a House of Lords and Ladies. If that should happen, it would surely be the unanimous wish of the people that the heiress to the throne should be the first of her sex to take her seat and assume the ancient position of the heir at the head of the lay peerage. Indeed one may suppose that in those circumstances the Prime Minister of the day would formally advise His Majesty to confer upon his daughter a peerage in her own right.

Which of the royal dukedoms would be chosen for such a purpose is a matter for the taste of the two exalted personages concerned, though no doubt their taste would be guided by history. There are three that have claims to be considered. Clarence, which was borne by a comparatively recent heir presumptive, afterwards William IV, and most recently by the elder brother of King George V, has the most venerable history, going back through the great feudal house of Clare to the morrow of the Norman Conquest. Cumberland, as has been said, is the only peerage title that has belonged to a future queen regnant of England. Its last English holder was Ernest, fifth son of King George III, who, on the death of his brother William, succeeded to the Kingdom of Hanover as heir male under the Salic Law, while his niece Victoria, daughter of his elder brother, inherited England as heir general under the Act of Settlement. Thereafter the Dukedom of Cumberland became merged in this German kingdom, and was extinguished by Act of Parliament during the First World War. The third probable peerage is the Dukedom of York, which, being by custom given to the King's second son, has been held by most of the male heirs presumptive in English history. Edward IV, Henry VIII, Charles I, James II, George V and George VI were all in their time Dukes of York, and nothing could be more in accord with the spirit of English history than the assumption some day by Princess Elizabeth of the dignity that her father and grandfather before her have endeared to the people.

But all these things are but the outward trappings of princely estate, empty in themselves, though full of significance if they are understood as helping to place Princess Elizabeth in the long succession of queens and heirs to which she belongs, and to symbolize the subtle relationship that unites her with the people over whom she will some day reign. Clothed then in the traditions that have descended to her from so many bygone men and women who have once occupied positions partly resembling hers, yet also born to circumstances that are in so many ways unique, the Princess—who is today the most important young woman of her age in the world—may be expected to make for herself a brilliant place in the life of the nation during the many years that all hope will pass before she is called to her high destiny.

VICTORY DRIVE—8th JUNE, 1946

CHRISTENING GROUP—29th MAY, 1926

LIFE STORY OF
THE PRINCESS : (I) CHILDHOOD

ON 20th April, 1926, Sir William Joynson-Hicks, Secretary of State for Home Affairs in Mr. Baldwin's second government, was summoned to No. 17 Bruton Street, in the west end of London, the home of Lord and Lady Strathmore. His journey was made in obedience to ancient custom, and called up memories of a famous constitutional crisis of two and a half centuries before. In July, 1688, Queen Mary of Modena, second wife of King James II, whose previous children had died in infancy, and who had long been thought incapable of having another, gave birth prematurely to the son who was afterwards to be known to the Whigs as the Old Pretender, and to the Jacobites as King James III and VIII. The event, in that age of ruthless party conflict, became the occasion of ferocious controversy, for the birth of a son who would be brought up as a papist was hailed by the one side and execrated by the other as extinguishing the hopes of the eventual accession of the King's Protestant daughter, Mary of Orange, to the throne. The infuriated Whigs soon put about a story that the child was no son of the King and Queen, but a base-born brat which had been surreptitiously introduced into the Queen's bedchamber in a warming pan. No serious historian, even the most bigoted Whig, has ever seriously believed in the so-called warming-pan plot; as a matter of fact, the unhappy Queen went through her ordeal in a room crowded to suffocation with eminent persons of both sexes. But it is true that for various reasons some of the people who would normally be present, such as the Archbishop of Canterbury (who was in prison), were not there; and it was alleged that the King had deliberately packed the room with his own partisans, who might be trusted to perjure themselves in furtherance of his plot. In subsequent times, accordingly, it has become stereotyped custom that a minister constitutionally responsible to Parliament should be present in an adjoining room, as an unchallengeable witness, at the birth of any child who by any

possibility of law might one day accede to the throne. It was on this mission that Sir William Joynson-Hicks came to No. 17 Bruton Street, where Lord Strathmore's youngest daughter, Elizabeth, Duchess of York, was expecting the birth of her first child.

The event that was about to take place in Bruton Street was surrounded with an atmosphere strangely contrasting with that in St. James's Palace so many years before. The Home Secretary, though in constitutional form he was an umpire in case of the outbreak of such another violent dispute as that of 1688, came in spirit as the first representative of a united people wholeheartedly rejoicing in the beginning of another generation of a much loved Royal Family. The time was peculiarly apt for the occurrence of what was, in something more than the perfunctory sense, "a happy event." The country was passing through a dark period. The patriotic exaltation, which had carried the people triumphantly through the tragic years of the First World War, had petered out in a slough of depression and disillusion, and a long phase of industrial disunion was to culminate within a few days in the outbreak of the General Strike. Something over which all ranks of a divided people could unite to rejoice, because it spoke to them of the future in which these passing dissensions might be transcended, was therefore a much-needed stimulus to the flagging spirits of the nation.

It was not, indeed, with any immediate thought of a future sovereign that the British Empire looked forward to this birth. The Prince of Wales was not yet thirty-two; he might reasonably be expected to marry and become the father of children, all of whom, whether boys or girls, would stand nearer to the succession than any who might be born to his brother. The child to be born would therefore be taken to the heart of the nation simply for what she already was, rather than for what by a possibility then remote she might conceivably become. There was a

ON QUEEN MARY'S KNEE—MAY, 1926

MOTHER AND DAUGHTER—1927

place to be filled. King George V was over sixty. His children were grown up. But the Royal Family has become by universal sentiment the representative family of the Commonwealth; and a family can scarcely be representative without possessing a nursery. If the King had no young children, so the people instinctively thought, he ought to have grandchildren. He had, indeed, two already, but the sons of the Princess Royal were naturally regarded as belonging less to the Royal Family proper than to the noble house into which she had married. The appearance of a second generation in the male line would be a kind of completion of the Royal Family.

The girl who was born at three o'clock in the morning on 21st April took her place at once in the hearts of the people, by virtue not only of her place in the Royal Family, but also of the great personal popularity of her parents. They had never sought any spectacular public position. On the contrary, they seemed deliberately to have made their own the most laborious and least conspicuous tasks in the wide range of public service that devolves upon the Royal Family, leaving all the limelight, as was constitutionally proper, to the heir to the throne. The Duke of York had devoted himself to the traditionally silent service of the Navy, to the bringing together of widely separated social classes among the young, and to the furtherance of happy relations in industrial life. But it was precisely this self-sacrificing immersion in work-a-day things that gained him recognition as an outstanding labourer for the people's best interests at this time of social uncertainty and disquiet. He had made himself a link between the large and stately ideas of national greatness, which it is a major function of royalty to make visible, and the hard realities of daily life which have to be faced and mastered if the state and the glory are not to become a mockery and a sham.

In addition, the popularity of the Duke and Duchess was magnified by the universal recognition that their marriage had been a love match. It marked the emancipation of the Royal Family from a tradition of political and dynastic alliances, which to many people had always been distasteful, and in the circumstances of the modern world had become manifestly out of date. Even King George V never did a more popular thing than when he gladly gave his consent to the marriage

HAPPY RETURN. *In January, 1927, the Duke and Duchess of York left for Australia on an official tour, leaving their baby daughter in the care of her grandparents the Earl and Countess of Strathmore. On their return in June there was a family reunion at Buckingham Palace. Above, the reunited family are seen waving their greetings to the enthusiastic crowd from the balcony of their Piccadilly home.*

CHILDHOOD STUDY—1928

of his second son to one of his own subjects—and one indeed whose marriage could by no stretch of imagination be held to have political significance. The Duchess's parents were simple Scottish people, who devoted themselves, as became their station, to the welfare of the people among whom they lived, but had never sought to play any part upon the stage of national or international affairs. The family, however, had no cause to fear comparison with the princely houses of the Continent, which had furnished so many royal brides. According to the accepted canons of genealogy the house of Bowes-Lyon can look back on its ancestry with no less pride than the Royal Family itself; for Glamis Castle has descended in an unbroken male line for nearly six hundred years, which is very far from being true of Windsor.

The history of this much respected Scottish family begins, as in our time it has culminated, in a royal marriage. John Lyon, one of the ablest Scottish officers of state in the later Middle Ages, having served King David II from 1369 as a diplomatist and ultimately chamberlain, in 1376 secretly married Lady Jean Stewart, the widowed daughter of David's successor, Robert II. The marriage was very soon avowed; and the

TRICYCLE RIDE—1930

IN THE GARDEN, 145 PICCADILLY—1928

King conferred upon his "dear son" the honour of knighthood and considerable estates; to which Sir John's descendants, devoting themselves through many generations to the royal service, steadily added. His grandson Patrick became, in 1445, the first Lord Glamis. Another Patrick, the ninth Lord Glamis, was created in 1606 Earl of Kinghorne, and his grandson, Patrick, the third earl, surrendered this dignity to the Crown, to be re-invested as Earl of Strathmore and Kinghorne, receiving several new baronies in addition. John, the fifth earl, still faithful to the house of Stuart, whom his family had served for three and a half centuries, joined the standard of "King James VIII" in 1715 and was killed at the Battle of Sheriffmuir; but he was not attainted, and the family honours descended in turn to his three brothers, Charles, James and Thomas. By 1745 the family had become reconciled to the Hanoverian dynasty, and were not involved in the rebellion of that year. John, the ninth earl, married in 1776 the heiress of the Durham family of Bowes of Streatlam Castle, and for a time the family took her name. His son for the first time added an English peerage to the family's long list of Scottish dignities, becoming Lord Bowes

SKIRL O' THE PIPES—GLAMIS, 1929

in the year of Waterloo; but he died without issue and this title accordingly lapsed. It was revived in 1887 for his nephew, Claude, the thirteenth earl, who reasserted the ancient tradition of the family by reverting to the name of Bowes-Lyon instead of Lyon-Bowes. His son, Claude George, father of the Duchess of York, was fourteenth Earl of Strathmore and Kinghorne and twenty-second Lord Glamis in the peerage of Scotland, and represented a continuous tradition which only

They will prefer to step aside into the female but British line with Queen Victoria, who was the granddaughter of King George III; and he was in turn the great-grandson of King George I. Here again, if we care to follow the male line of ancestry, we shall come through the Electors of Brunswick into the records of another German princely family, this time a younger line of the mighty house of Guelph. In European history few dynasties who were never sovereign have

FIRST MEET WITH THE PYTCHLEY HOUNDS—14th APRIL 1931

a handful of families in the three kingdoms can surpass or even match.

The Royal Family is not one of them. Its tradition is indeed as continuous as it is majestic; but its continuity is that of history, not of genealogy. If we pursue Princess Elizabeth's ancestry backwards through the strictly male line, as is the genealogical convention, we come four generations back to her great-great-grandfather, Albert of Saxe-Coburg-Gotha; and if we wish to go further we shall lose ourselves in the annals of a German princely house of the second rank, cadets of the royal family of Saxony. That is not the direction in which the main interest of Princess Elizabeth's pedigree lies for her future subjects.

played so potent a part as these; and it is interesting that in the twelfth and thirteenth centuries the great Guelph confederation, which in the main supported the Papacy against the Empire, was closely associated with English dynastic alliances, Duke Henry the Lion, the proud and turbulent head of the house, being a son-in-law of our King Henry II. Much play was made with these old associations when the Guelph King George I came to England in 1714; but the reader will prefer again to turn from the German branches of the Princess's ancestry, and follow the line that leads back into the annals of Britain.

That line is traced through George's mother, the Electress Sophia, of whom something has

AT TROOPING THE COLOUR—JUNE, 1931

been said in the introduction; and she in turn was the daughter of Elizabeth, Queen of Bohemia, with whose father, King James VI of Scotland and I of England we return to the British Isles. King James therefore is the only one of the Stuart sovereigns of England who stands in Princess Elizabeth's ancestry. Through him and his mother, Mary, of course, she descends from both the old English and Scottish royal lines. Mary Queen of Scots was the daughter of James V, who was the lineal descendant of Robert, Hereditary High Steward of Scotland, who became King in 1371 as Robert II in right of his mother, Marjorie Bruce, the daughter and eventual heiress of the patriot victor of the Battle of Bannockburn. Robert Bruce, in his turn, descends by a junior branch from King David I in the twelfth century, the main line of the Scottish Kings having come to an end, as every schoolboy remembers, with the death of its heiress, Margaret the Maid of

Norway, on her voyage home to Scotland in 1290. Behind King David stretches away the long shadowy line of the McAlpine Kings, including Shakespeare's Duncan, until it is lost in the mists of legend, where we dimly descry one Fergus Mor McErc, said to have come from Ireland as first King of the Scots of Dalriada in 498.

Returning to the sixteenth century, King James V of Scotland was, through his mother, Margaret Tudor, a grandson of King Henry VII of England, who had united the White and Red Roses by his marriage with Elizabeth of York. His own ancestry, although he did descend in an ambiguous way from John of Gaunt, is really less important than that of his wife. She was the daughter of King Edward IV, the heir of the Dukes of York, whose claim to the throne, however, was not derived from their male ancestor, the first Duke, who was only the fourth son of King Edward III, but from their ancestress, Anne Mortimer, great-

ARRIVING AT GLAMIS WITH HER NEW SISTER—AUGUST, 1931

AT ST. PAUL'S, WALDEN BURY—1932

granddaughter and heiress of Lionel Duke of Clarence, the second son. The line of the Black Prince (eldest son of Edward III) having expired with Richard II in 1339, Lionel's descendants represented the senior line of the kings known to after ages, but not to themselves, as Plantagenet. It is a relief to emerge from the tangled genealogies of the fifteenth century and resume the clear line which runs straight back from the first three Edwards, Henry III and John, to the great King Henry II in 1159. Henry II in the male line derives from the Counts of Anjou, who can be followed back to one Tortulf the Forester in the ninth century, of whom history knows no more than the name. But Henry's mother was the daughter of Henry I and a granddaughter of William the Conqueror. She was also the daughter of the Scottish Princess Margaret, who by her marriage with Henry I brought back to conquered England the old Anglo-Saxon royal line; being the great-granddaughter of the heroic Edmund Ironside, who fought the last fight against the conquering Danes and was himself fifth in descent from Alfred the Great. So the illustrious line goes back through Egbert, sometimes called the first King of United

England, to Cerdic, who is said to have led the first West Saxon war bands to Britain in the fifth century, and at last, if the family's own records are to be believed, to the god Odin himself.

These are some of the mighty and romantic ancestors of the baby girl at No. 17 Bruton Street who confronted the Secretary of State and is reported to have yawned at the presentation.

In accordance with the traditional privilege of the City, the first person outside the house to whom the news was sent was the Lord Mayor of London; and at breakfast time it was known to newspaper readers throughout the land. Messages of congratulation to the King and the young parents flowed in from all over the Empire and, indeed, the whole world; and for a time, as was to be expected, the papers gave detailed but not very startling information about the daily progress of the small Princess. Gradually the excitement waned. Fascinating as the first steps of a newcomer in life will always be to those who have a direct interest in the child— and all the King's subjects felt such an interest in this child—they are steps that have been taken before, and even the most illustriously descended infant finds it impossible to give them an original or specially princely turn. And this infant after all did not seem to be marked out for any major place in history. Even supposing that her uncle should choose to maintain his bachelor state, there was a reasonable chance that she would some day have a brother, who would in due course become her Sovereign, and that she herself would ultimately marry some eminent subject of the King, and become the ancestress of a family that would merge itself with the people of the land. Certainly, the Duke and Duchess of York had no desire that their baby daughter should become a public figure to any greater degree than was unavoidable. No pomp and circumstance, for instance, attended her christening, which was privately carried out in the chapel at Buckingham Palace when she was five weeks old. The gold vessel, known as the Lily Font, which was designed in 1840 for Queen Victoria's first child, was brought from Windsor and filled with water from the River Jordan, according to a custom going back to the Crusades. With this water of the stream in

which the first recorded baptisms were celebrated, the little Princess was baptized by the late Dr. Lang, then Archbishop of York, receiving the name Elizabeth Alexandra Mary. The sponsors were the four grandparents, the Princess Royal and the Duke of Connaught, the last of them a remarkable link with the past, for at his own christening the godfather after whom he was named was Arthur, the great Duke of Wellington, who had been born in 1769.

Of the three names conferred upon the Princess the significance needs no explanation. She was called Mary after her grandmother, the Queen, Alexandra after her great-grandmother; for the choice of Elizabeth it would be artificial to suggest any other reason than that it was her mother's name. It was none the less a happy coincidence that the child who was to be called to such greatness should bear what must be to every Englishman the queenliest of names.

For the first three months of her life the little Princess remained in her grandparents' home in Bruton Street, while the crowds stood outside to

ABERGELDIE FAIR—1933

try to catch a glimpse of her. But within, time flowed quietly over the generally unconscious head. For, like babies of less exalted rank, the Princess Elizabeth spent most of her days asleep. The industrial troubles of that unhappy year dragged themselves out to their close; they did not trouble her, however much they may have saddened the heart of that other grandparent, King George V, who many times broke away from the anxieties of kingship to come and pay homage, like any plebeian to the new symbol of the hopes of the future. For the King, known to all his Empire as the most fatherly of monarchs, threw himself with delight into the part of a grandfather. To watch the growth of the little girl who would some day, though he did not know it, sit upon his throne, was perhaps the greatest joy of his later years; and Queen Mary was not less ready to play the part of the devoted grandmother and take the child to her heart.

They had to part with her, however, for a short time when she reached the age of three months and went to stay at the home of her mother's childhood, the famous Castle of Glamis, which is said to be the oldest inhabited house in the British Isles. The main part dates from the time of Patrick the first earl, at the turn of the sixteenth and seventeenth centuries. It is a place of imposing but rather grim fortifications, where it is easy to believe the legends of haunted rooms and mysterious terrifying secrets, handed down from father to son, which are among the classic ghost stories of Scotland. There is much there to recall the heroic and blood-stained story of Scotland's kings; but the relics are mainly memorials of a lost cause. In the chapel the figure of Christ is painted in the likeness of King Charles I. In the entrance hall hangs the coat of Graham of Claverhouse, known in ballad as Bonny Dundee. A watch left behind in 1746 recalls that, although the Lyons of that day had resigned themselves at last to Hanoverian rule, there was enough of the older loyalty left to make their castle a sanctuary for a few days of Prince Charlie's wanderings. Here, in fact, still survives the memory and the atmosphere of the old allegiance; and the little girl gradually awakening in its shadow to the full consciousness of life, the child in whose veins flowed the blood both of Stuart and of Hanover, was in her own person an emblem of the reconciliation that comes at last to soften the memories of "old unhappy far off things and battles long ago."

It was, indeed, in the shadow only of those frowning walls that the baby passed her earliest days, for the more venerable, imposing, and sometimes forbidding buildings, containing apartments with such sombre names as "The Hangman's Room," are not now the home of daily life. There is a modern wing, rebuilt in the last century, looking out on a pleasant Dutch garden, which is Lady Strathmore's personal creation and care; and here in an atmosphere of light and peace the Princess made her first acquaintance with Scotland.

In mid-autumn the Duke and Duchess with their daughter came back to London and remained at Buckingham Palace until it was time for the whole Royal Family to go off together to spend their Christmas holiday at Sandringham. This pleasant Norfolk country house was always the favourite home of King George V, and he loved to slip back there into the position of squire among his tenantry rather than the King Emperor of innumerable subjects. The little curly-headed girl, who by this time was crawling at an ever accelerating pace up and down the passages, completed by her presence the atmosphere proper to an English family Christmas. It was a merrier time for the King and Queen than perhaps they had enjoyed since the last of their children had grown up; but for the Duke and Duchess the merriment was not without an undercurrent of sadness. The service that the country expects of all the Royal Family, and that is always rendered devotedly and without question, has often to be given at the cost of a sacrifice not demanded of humbler folk. The Commonwealth of Australia was about to celebrate the institution of its new capital at Canberra, and had petitioned the King to send out his second son as his representative to preside over the ceremonies of inauguration and to open the first Canberra Parliament in state. The Princess was adjudged too young to travel half way round the world. In a less exalted family no doubt the father would have performed the mission alone, while the mother remained behind to marvel at the miracles of the first months of baby life, for which nothing in later years can altogether compensate. But this mission of the Duke of York was something more than a state ceremonial. Australian loyalty required

BRIDESMAID AT DUKE OF KENT'S WEDDING—29th NOVEMBER, 1934

A JUBILEE AND A WEDDING. *On 6th May, 1935, King George V and Queen Mary celebrated their Silver Jubilee and the Royal Family attended a thanksgiving service in St. Paul's Cathedral. Above, the King, Queen, and members of the Royal Family are seen on the balcony of Buckingham Palace after the service. Below*

(left), the two Princesses are leaving the Cathedral with their parents and the Duke and Duchess of Kent. In the following November, the Duke of Gloucester married Lady Alice Scott, when Princess Elizabeth was again a bridesmaid. Below (right), she is seen bidding goodbye to the newly married couple as they left on their honeymoon.

OUT RIDING WITH HER UNCLE IN WINDSOR GREAT PARK—1935

the presence of a representative of the Queen as well as the King, to be the centre of the national rejoicing, and the Duchess, at whatever cost in human feeling, had to tear herself away from the nursery which had become the focus of her life. The baby remained at Buckingham Palace, every day consolidating her dominion over the hearts of her grandparents, learning to walk and to form her first words, and posing repeatedly for photographers, professional and amateur; for her young parents twelve thousand miles away insisted upon receiving fresh pictures by every mail. That does not mean quite so much as it would today, for the air route to Australia had not yet been mapped out; but at least they were doing all that was within human power to watch through the eye of the camera the fascinating progress they so much longed to see.

They were not the only ones who were watching with the mind's eye. Australia was quite as much excited over the newcomer to the Royal Family as was the mother country; and from every part of the Commonwealth gifts of toys of all shapes and sizes came pouring in. When at last H.M.S. *Renown* sailed from Perth on the return journey room had to be found for over three tons of Her Royal Highness's property—including some score of live parrots.

Meanwhile two sets of grandparents had been in amicable rivalry for the enjoyment of the baby's company. The settlement reached was that she should divide her time equally between the two families; and with characteristic courtesy King George permitted the subject's claim to be satisfied before the Sovereign's. So off went the Princess to spend the first half of her six months as a temporary orphan with Lady Strathmore at her English country home at St. Paul's, Walden Bury, in Hertfordshire. In contrast to the stern grandeur of Glamis Castle this red brick house of Queen Anne's date breathed suggestions of nothing but the simplest, kindliest, and most fragrant aspects of English country life. Here was no majesty of historic association; and yet there was the mellowness and peace that come only in the midst of a people to whom the centuries have brought ripeness and harmony. It was winter time now; and so Princess Elizabeth could not yet bask in the sunny gardens, with their oak trees and mulberries and elaborate topiary, their roses and their bees, which would be a delight in many later summers

TATTOO REHEARSAL.
Princess Elizabeth received by
the officer of the guard when
she arrived with her sister
for the dress rehearsal of the
Aldershot Tattoo in June, 1935.

of childhood. But she could inherit her mother's own nursery, and make the adventurous transition from progress on all fours to the dignity of the upright posture in the midst of the story-book pictures that had been hung round the walls to frame the childhood of the ten Bowes-Lyon boys and girls of a generation before. It is in these sanctuaries of unpretentious family life that time seems most gracefully to stand still as the generations repeat themselves; and the illusion was the more perfect at St. Paul's because the Duchess's own nurse, Miss Knight, was still there to take charge of another Elizabeth. Hers was a trust of momentous import to a great Empire, although it is unlikely that her name will appear prominently in any history book, and although she certainly did not receive any instrument of appointment corresponding to the solemn letters patent which King Henry VI at the age of nine months granted under the Great Seal to his nurse, Dame Alice Butler, "with licence reasonably to chastise us" if the occasion should require. It is well sometimes for a people who owe so great a part of the unique harmony of their national life to the service rendered by royalty to reflect for a moment on the profound influence that may be exerted, through their Kings and Queens upon themselves, by unknown men and women who have guided the future wearers of crowns through their earliest and most impressionable years. It is the peculiar good fortune of the English that there is always an abundance of men and women of simple and upright character who can undertake in obscurity the tasks of which the consequences will become of world-wide significance, though their own contribution will be forgotten; and among these Miss Knight is entitled to an honourable place, as the first of a succession of tried and trusted friends who have helped their future Sovereign on her way.

Most small children have a tendency, sometimes disconcerting to the self-esteem of their elders, to exalt their four-footed to at least an equal place with their human friends. It seems to have been during this stay at St. Paul's, Walden, that the Princess made her first acquaintance with the world of dogs, here represented by two large and amiable chows, one black and one brown, which after the manner of their kind submitted with an astonishingly good grace to the indiscriminate mauling of baby hands. They were the first of an endless succession of pets which were to become an indispensable part of the Princess's life; she was a dog lover from infancy, and very soon a horse lover as well; and many photographs in this book lend support

LEAVING CRATHIE CHURCH WITH HER GRANDFATHER—AUGUST, 1935

to the view that the time she spends with animals includes some of the happiest hours of her life.

The three months at St. Paul's, Walden, however, came to an end, and the King and Queen carried off their granddaughter to Buckingham Palace. She was now nearly a year old, and beginning to be a distinguishable figure in human society. She began to be aware of her two cousins, George and Gerald Lascelles, both a little older than herself, who came to tea and gave her the chance to practise the new art of conversation. She had not many words yet; but she was learning to say "Mummie" in preparation for an important meeting now drawing near; she even accomplished what many historians would have thought an impossibility by finding a new variant upon the manifold versions of her own name. She took to calling herself "Lilibet," and the charming liquid syllables soon became inseparably attached to her on the lips of her family and friends.

About the time that H.M.S. *Renown* was steaming out of Port Melbourne the Princess moved into a home of her own, and indeed, in the absence of her parents, might be held to have attained the dignity of temporary head of the household. Number 145 Piccadilly had been acquired as a town residence for the Duke and Duchess of York; and before leaving for Australia the Duchess had herself devoted much time and care to the fitting up of the nursery floor. It was at the top of the house, where the rooms opened on a circular landing under a glass dome; a landing that could be made at will a racecourse or a stage, and above all a vantage point from which baby eyes could get a perfect view of the coming and going of the innumerable visitors— some of them great figures in the life of the nation—who crossed the entrance hall far below to be entertained by the Duke and Duchess of York. The nurseries had their own kitchen, and

Y BWTHYN BACH. *"The Little House" was presented to Princess Elizabeth on her sixth birthday by the people of Wales. It was erected in the gardens of the Royal Lodge at Windsor where, in 1936, this photograph was taken.*

OUTSIDE "THE LITTLE HOUSE." *The Royal Family are great dog lovers as is shown by this picture taken in front of Y Bwthyn Bach in 1936. Two corgis, a Tibetan lion dog and a Labrador complete the family group.*

everything was arranged to provide a self-contained life for the little community of which the Princess was the centre. Behind the house was a small garden, and when that did not suffice there was the whole of Hyde Park to walk in; at least there would have been, had it not been found very quickly that public interest in the Princess was far too great to allow her to take her walks undistracted. The crowds that flocked round the perambulator wherever it went soon became unmanageable; and the Princess was for the most part driven back on the garden, although her innumerable admirers still managed to catch an occasional glimpse through the railings which were all that divided it from the park.

And so at last the long separation—for be it remembered that six months were nearly half the Princess's lifetime up to date, and by that time scale they must be measured—came to an end. On the afternoon of 27th June the little girl was dressed in her brightest clothes and taken across to Buckingham Palace, where the seething crowds round the gates no doubt conveyed to her that for some reason this was no ordinary occasion. She did not yet know that the cheers of many thousand people are not the ordinary accompaniment when any little girl meets her parents again after a long separation; but when eventually the royal car drove in from Victoria Station and the Duchess seized her daughter in her arms, the re-union was not to be distinguished from any similar happy scene.

Afterwards the three tons of toys were unloaded and brought for the inspection of their fortunate owner. Some of them were taken to her heart, and went to crowd the shelves of the toy cupboard at 145 Piccadilly. Even royal hands, however, delighting in destruction as do those of all small children, could scarcely work through so vast a supply; and a large proportion of these multitudinous gifts soon found its way to children's hospitals and other charities. No doubt the

CORONATION DAY. *The Duke of Norfolk, Earl Marshal of England, received Princess Elizabeth when she arrived at Westminster Abbey to attend the Coronation of her parents in that historic building on 12th May, 1937.*

LEAVING THE ABBEY. *After the Coronation ceremony the two Princesses, wearing their coronets and walking hand-in-hand with bowed heads, immediately preceded Queen Mary from the Abbey in the ceremonial procession.*

ROYAL VISIT TO EDINBURGH. In July, 1937, the Royal Family paid an official visit to Edinburgh. Here they are arriving at the Castle for the ceremony of handing over the keys.

WITH THE ROYAL BODYGUARD. *During his visit to Scotland the King inspected the Royal Company of Archers, his bodyguard for Scotland, at Holyrood Palace, Edinburgh. Above, with the Queen and the two Princesses, he is seen in conversation with members of this famous company.*

generous-hearted donors would understand. Even from infancy the members of the Royal Family are first and foremost representatives of their subjects, *the people*; and the gifts they receive are given by implication to the people with whom they are at one. To pass on their presents where they will be most appreciated is the right and royal expression of gratitude.

But far more precious to a baby princess than a regiment of teddy bears was the restoration of a devoted mother and father, whom she could now begin to know as living and loving human creatures, and not as the mere elemental forces that they must presumably have appeared in cradle days, or as the remote and scarcely comprehended names that they had been during those six months of separation. For several years now the efforts of the Duke and Duchess would be devoted to securing for their daughter the sort of natural, homely, and intimate nursery life that every little girl ought to enjoy, and to prevent the innumerable claims that ceremonial and public life made upon themselves from breaking in upon her and disturbing the natural tenor of her days.

The Duchess was insistent that no one but the Princess's mother should direct and supervise every detail of her upbringing. The best of nurses were there to help, but were no substitute for a mother's personal affection and care. So, in spite of all the demands that are made upon royal persons even if outside the direct line of succession, it was the Duchess herself who told the Princess the old familiar fairy tales and nursery rhymes that are the common inheritance of prince and peasant, and it was she who in due course guided her through the first formidable mysteries of the ABC. The Duke, still more beset with the manifold preoccupations of his public life, was no less determined to devote every possible moment to watching and participating in the endlessly fascinating process that gradually transformed the passive helplessness of babyhood into a person in her own right with a character, a temper, a will, and very definite tastes and capacities of her own.

She was very much a person by the time she was two and a half; and she was even capable then of performing, though she did not know it, a

THREE ROYAL LADIES—1937

WITH "DOOKIE" AT GLAMIS—1937

public service to the Commonwealth. That was the time, at the end of 1928, when the almost desperate illness of King George V kept the whole Empire for many weeks under the persistent shadow of imminent loss. When at last the crisis was surmounted, and he went away to recover his strength slowly in the sea air of Bognor, it was at his special request that his little granddaughter was invited to keep him company; and it is easy to believe that her sunny vitality and her loving nature contributed much to the re-establishment of his health.

Sick or hale, the old King, whom the Princess generally addressed as "Grandpapa England" was always the devoted slave of his granddaughter, would meekly accept the imperious commands or devastating rebukes that the very young habitually deal out to their elders, and would spend hours playing nursery games little suggestive of the pomp and dignity proper to the King's Majesty. He was, however, only one of four grandparents, and all of them combined to surround the Princess with the environment of an idyllic childhood. She travelled backwards and

forwards through the range of delightful homes with which their united resources could provide her: to Buckingham Palace and Windsor Castle, to Sandringham, Balmoral and Birkhall, and to the various houses of the Bowes-Lyon family at Glamis or St. Paul's, Walden Bury, in Hertfordshire. All these houses had their own distinctive characters, all of them were steeped in the rich traditions of England or Scotland; but it was probably not the bricks or stones that made for the Princess the essential environment of her earliest life. It was to the gardens and the woods that she most intimately belonged. She was preeminently a creature of the open air, nearly always in rapid motion, delighting in her own early attempts at gardening, romping with innumerable dogs, and before she was four years old acquiring her first Shetland pony, named Peggy, and taking her first lessons in riding from Owen, the King's stud groom.

All this might have been the lot of any child born into a family fortunate enough to have access to big country houses and spacious gardens scattered up and down the land. The Duke and Duchess had no desire that the Princess should have anything more; but with the best intentions her royal position could not be prevented from occasionally bringing her its own heady excitements. There were soldiers, for instance. When a very small girl discovers that the imposing scarlet guardsman at the gate will go through the stately exercise known as "presenting arms" every time she chances to pass the sentry box, she would not be human if she did not set the clashing machinery at work over and over again. So also it was an excitement when the Princess discovered that grown-up ladies would sink to the earth before her in the ceremonious gesture of the curtsey; but this came rather later in life.

She was rather more than four years old when the first great transformation occurred in the nursery world. On 21st August, 1930, she was told that a baby sister had arrived to keep her company, and looked out from the tall windows of Glamis to see the night sky spangled with fire, as beacons were lit to carry the news over Scotland. It was the beginning of a companionship more happy and devoted than is common among sisters, more particularly when there is a considerable gap between their ages. The elder immediately took the newcomer to her heart,

GIRL GUIDE REVIEW. *On 19th June, 1938, the two Princesses made their first official appearance in uniform when the King and Queen reviewed 1,000 Girl Guides at Windsor Castle. Above, Princess Margaret is trying to replace her sister's sheath knife which the King had playfully "stolen" from her belt.*

heaping her own toys on the baby's cot; and almost from the first up to the present time her sister has been by far her most intimate friend.

Thereafter followed the process of new adaptations which every eldest child has to undergo when it ceases to be alone in the nursery and becomes, instead of a diminutive autocrat, no more than a member of a community of two, and that not the member about whom the greater fuss is made. The disturbing experience goes on inarticulately, within the recesses of childish personality, and is forgotten before the subject is of an age to tell the world about it. All that can be said about this particular example of an almost universal experience is that Princess Elizabeth passed through the revolution of her world without a sign of inward turmoil. She has never been self-centred or much concerned with her own importance; and from the first she saw her little sister far more as a companion and playfellow than as a rival. Life was now doubled in interest, because two small minds, with the world opening out its romantic possibilities before them, could share and discuss every new aspect of its limitless prospects. There was someone to play with, someone to race with, and of course someone that it was only human nature to quarrel with occasionally; but all this in the intimacy of a little world of her own, distinct from the mysterious country of grown-ups, who with the best intentions can never quite get beyond the character of exceedingly friendly aliens.

New dignities, becoming to the position of an elder sister, were now beginning to descend upon the Princess. She acquired for the first time a tartan kilt. About the time of Princess Margaret's birth she made her first appearance in the Court Circular, which announced that Her Royal Highness the Princess Elizabeth was staying with Their Majesties at Balmoral, as was also the Right Honourable Ramsay Macdonald, Prime Minister and First Lord of the Treasury. She was present at an important ceremony, the christening of the little sister, which took place like her own in the Chapel at Buckingham Palace. The Lily Font was brought out again, and Princess Elizabeth's own christening robe of Brussels lace was now worn by the newcomer, whose name is as historic in the history of the Scottish Royal Family as that of Elizabeth in the English; for it comes down from her remote ancestress the canonized saint Margaret, the wife of King Malcolm Canmore. Before long the two children were able to assert their individuality in the public eye by having a Court Circular all to themselves: "Balmoral, September 19, 1931. The Princess Elizabeth and the Princess Margaret of York have left the Castle."

This coming and going to and from other people's houses—for after all the stately abodes of even the most affectionate grandparents were not in the full sense home—began henceforth to be regularly announced in the public Press. But the Duke and Duchess of York, with two children now to bring up, were feeling the need for a house of their own in the country; and in 1932 they accordingly took over Royal Lodge in Windsor Great Park. This was one of the houses originally built for the Prince Regent by the great architect Nash, whose fine and spacious workmanship is still familiar to all Londoners in such ranges as the great terraces of Regent's Park. Most of the original house, however, has now been pulled down and rebuilt; nor does any satisfactory description or picture survive to tell us what Royal Lodge was like in 1814. We know, however, that it was a specimen of the romantic antiquarianism of the day, with the reed-thatched roof and mullioned windows which, to the Waterloo generation, stood for "Gothick" charm. It became the favourite headquarters of the Regent for Ascot races, and a place of retirement when he became King. Rebuilt in a less pretentious but probably more comfortable style, it was in 1932 a place of retirement still: an unassuming family home, quite small by the rather formidable standards of royal residences, and above all set in complete seclusion, where two young children could forget that they were, whether they would or not, eminent public characters. Here they could throw appearances to the winds, range untrammelled about their woods and gardens, and in their amusements come near to the likeness of the young savage who is the ideal and model of every healthy child. They could pursue this sort of life as the chiefs of a large and multifarious tribe, which at this time included their own ponies, two Welsh corgis, two Shetland collies, fifteen blue budgerigars, and two capricious fawns which might or might not permit themselves to be approached.

BIRTHDAY RIDE—21st APRIL, 1939.

AT THE LONDON ZOO. *During the absence of their parents in Canada and the United States in May and June, 1939, the Princesses paid several visits to the Zoo. They are here seen at the Penguin Pool (above), watching the antics of a baby panda (below), and enjoying a ride on an elephant (right).*

But if the rambling gardens of Royal Lodge were a place of emancipation and release, in another aspect the move there is associated with a beginning of servitude. Shades of the prison house begin to close even upon Princesses; and now that the elder was six, the claims of education were beginning to be taken seriously. She had already learned to read, under her mother's personal care. During 1931 she had begun dancing lessons, and her teacher Miss Vacani has left it on record that she has never had a quicker pupil. It was probably in these dancing classes, which she shared with half a dozen other little girls at Number 145 Piccadilly, that the first clear signs were shown of the intense power of concentration which is a prominent feature of the Princess's character. What she does she does with all her might; and once she has attempted anything new, from a dance step upwards, she will not leave it alone until it is mastered. Rather later in the progress of the classes Princess Margaret was frequently her sister's partner; but the first steps she had to watch from a wallflower's position on her nurse's lap.

By 1932 also Princess Elizabeth was already a competent horsewoman, and was going twice a week to the Bath Club to learn to swim. She had also had some French lessons from a visiting French governess. But formal education really dates from the arrival in the household of Miss Marion Crawford in October, 1933.

Miss Crawford was young, Scottish, attractive, and very human. She was quickly accepted by her two pupils as an ally and companion; and soon established herself, under the affectionate nickname of "Crawfie," as a trusted and indispensable friend of the whole Royal Family. But although kindliness and a complete understanding of a child's outlook on life are her leading characteristics, she has the high sense of intellectual discipline which is an honourable tradition of Scotland. Under her authority the Princess's life was reduced to a carefully regulated system. Its centre, when the family was in London, moved down from the nursery floor of Number 145 Piccadilly to the newly constituted schoolroom on the floor below. There were blackboards and maps ranged round the walls, and a small-sized desk was obtained for the pupil, to which a second would be added in a year or two's time. A timetable was worked out, and very good cause had to be shown before any departure from it was allowed.

It began at seven-thirty in the morning, when the Princess was dressed and had breakfast in the nursery. At nine o'clock she went down to visit her parents, a daily event that the growing pressure of their public duties was never, if it could be avoided, allowed to interrupt. But it lasted only a quarter of an hour. At nine-fifteen lessons began, and continued until eleven, at which time there was a break of half an hour. The morning was completed with another hour's lessons from eleven-thirty to twelve-thirty, and at a quarter past one Princess Elizabeth went down to luncheon with her parents, if they were at home. That in these early years was the end of book work for the day. The afternoon was always spent out of doors if weather permitted; when it did not, music or drawing lessons were fitted in. There was tea in the schoolroom at a quarter to five, and between five-thirty and six-thirty the Duchess insisted on enjoying the company of her children in her own sitting-room. Then came supper; and at a quarter past seven Princess Elizabeth went to bed, claiming at this time the elder sister's privilege of sitting up nearly an hour longer than Princess Margaret.

On the lighter side of life Princess Elizabeth acquired about this time one of the most remarkable toys ever presented to a little girl. It was called "Y Bwthyn Bach to Gwellt," which means "the little house with the straw roof"; and it came to the Princess as the gift of the Welsh people on her sixth birthday. The architect was Mr. Morgan Willmott, who had designed it throughout with mathematical exactitude, so as to reduce every detail of a typical Welsh cottage to the proportion in which a child of six stands to a full-grown woman. It was furnished throughout on the same scale; and in fact the only full-sized object in it was the stamp on the diminutive Deed of Gift which conveyed the property from the Welsh nation to Her Royal Highness the Princess Elizabeth of York—"hereinafter called the donee." This minute inconsistency was unavoidable, because the size of stamps is fixed by law.

With this purely personal home of her own, complete with running water laid on, with real clocks, electric light, and every accessory of grown-up life, the Princess could entertain her sister and her friends, and play with complete verisimilitude the part of an independent householder. The house which still stands in the grounds of Royal Lodge—though today it is only in the hall that the Princess can still stand upright—has its own garden, and was even male Sovereign would have appeared on horseback; so there is no particular reason in precedent why any future queen should show herself in equestrian state. The Princess from well before she was six years old was accustomed to ride furiously in Windsor Great Park; and both there

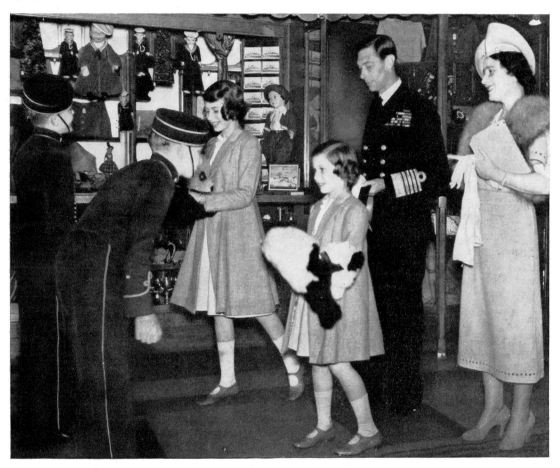

WELCOME HOME. *When the Princesses greeted their parents on their return from their tour of the United States and Canada on 22nd June, 1939, they were presented with toy pandas by members of the crew of the "Empress of Britain," the ship which had brought the King and Queen back to England.*

provided by the donors with its own watch dog, a thoroughbred Welsh terrier, named Ianto.

By this time the Princess was a very competent horsewoman and spent many long hours with or upon her pony. She ordinarily rode, and still rides, astride, but has learned to ride side-saddle as well; and no doubt if it is ever necessary for her to appear mounted on any ceremonial occasion she will adopt that more traditional and dignified mode. Queen Victoria, however, generally attended in her carriage on occasions when a

and in London both children have been familiar figures, riding on either side of their father's horse, although it has generally been necessary to get up very early in the morning in order to see them. Hunting however has played no great part in the Princess's life. She has been out with the Beaufort; and very early in her career, when she was only five, the Duke of York asked that she should be "blooded" with the Pytchley. But even a royal command cannot guarantee a kill, and her day ended in a clear victory for the fox.

For three or four years now the life of the Princess was mostly absorbed in the quiet routine of the schoolroom and the many open-air amusements which became ever more fascinating as her little sister became more nearly able to keep up with her.

In June, 1934, the Prince of Wales reached the age of forty. The pleasant game which had amused people for so many years of speculating on his matrimonial future had begun to lose its appeal, and it was gradually becoming accepted that he might well be a life-long bachelor after all. At the same time no little brother appeared in the Princesses' nursery. Consequently, the once remote possibility that Princess Elizabeth might some day be called to a dizzy eminence was now becoming more and more to be

SWIMMING ENTHUSIAST. *In July, 1939, the Princesses attended a swimming gala at Dartmouth (above). Princess Elizabeth, herself a keen swimmer, had won the Children's Challenge Shield at the Bath Club in the previous month. On the left she is seen "life-saving" during the competition.*

AT THE ROYAL AGRICULTURAL SHOW IN 1939

SINGING "THE CHESTNUT TREE." At the King's camp for boys from the public schools and the industrial areas, held at Abergeldie, near Balmoral, in August, 1939.

regarded as a probability. How soon the Royal Family in general, and the Duke and Duchess of York in particular, began to think of the Princess as a future Queen is their own secret. It must surely have been constantly present in their minds by this year of 1934, the year when the first ferocious outbursts of political murder by the new National Socialist government in Germany were giving dark forebodings of the terrible climate of the world in which the Princess was growing up. But if the Duke and Duchess foresaw by this time that their daughter would some day have to assume the leadership of the Empire in a world that by then might have been riven to its very foundations, they did not yet allow these ominous possibilities of the future to disturb the even tenor of her schoolroom days. They desired her to come to maturity under the same kindly influences as any little girl of private station, learning the ordinary lessons and playing the ordinary games, without any attempt to mould the natural course of education to the specialized responsibilities that might thereafter be laid upon her shoulders. In that policy they were ably and devotedly seconded by Miss Crawford. Everything was done to encourage the Princess to think of herself as an ordinary child; and the full success of that method of education is today perhaps her best qualification to become a Queen. For the first aim of modern constitutional monarchy is to set before the people a dedicated representative, in whose person they may feel that their own lives and interests, the simplicities of their natural character, are made incarnate. We expect nowadays that Tennyson's "white light that beats upon a throne" shall shine upon an ordinary man or woman, and make visible the virtue and the power that reside in ordinary human nature.

The public appearances that diversified these years of uneventful childhood were made mostly on purely family occasions. In November of 1934, for instance, the Princess was a bridesmaid in Westminster Abbey when her uncle George, Duke of Kent, married the Princess Marina of Greece. A year later she played a similar part at the wedding of Henry, Duke of Gloucester to Lady Alice Scott. Midway between these ceremonies, exciting as such occasions always

SANDRINGHAM—JANUARY, 1940

RIVER TRIP—JULY, 1940

are to right-minded little girls of eight or nine, came a larger and more solemn celebration. On 6th May, 1935, King George V and Queen Mary completed twenty-five years of a reign that had passed through years of danger and sorrow, through other years of doubt, difficulty, and internal dissension, and now seemed to be coming out at last into ways of pleasantness and peace. The love and loyalty of his people, which had grown ever more deep and powerful as the great reign ran its course, burst out at last on the anniversary in the most moving demonstration of the century. It was the Princess's first appearance in the processional pomp of royalty. The York family occupied the first of the royal carriages to leave Buckingham Palace for St. Paul's; and the two children, in their light pink frocks and straw hats, rather shyly waving their hands in response to the cheers of the crowd, were one of the pleasantest and most popular sights of that memorable day. In the Cathedral Princess Elizabeth sat on the right of her parents, just behind the King, while Princess Margaret had a big cushion at her mother's feet. With all the great personages of the realm assembled around them, to return humble thanks for all the deliverances and the blessings

of twenty-five years under King George's leadership, there must have come to the nine-year-old girl a new revelation of the other side of the affectionate easy-going grandfather who had always been so willing to indulge her baby whims. Here was a man who had laboured modestly and unceasingly through a lifetime in the service of others; and here, in the unanimous tribute now being paid by men and women representing every kind of genius and distinction, was the reward of the good and faithful servant. To this small girl, now beginning to be picked out from her contemporaries by the finger of destiny, her grandfather must have been seen that day as a supreme example that she might one day try to follow; and when later in the day she came out with the whole Royal Family on the balcony at Buckingham Palace, from which so many royal appearances have been made, the uncontrollable enthusiasm of the myriads of people who packed the great spaces below and reached back along the Mall almost to Admiralty Arch spoke to her, too, of a devotion that would some day be her inheritance.

The rejoicings of those sunlit days, which showed no sign of abating when the Government, a week after the Jubilee, were obliged to order their conclusion, were the last that King George V was to share with his people. He spoke to them once more indeed, in his Christmas broadcast, thanking them for what he called their warm and generous remembrance, which seems to have taken him, alone in his Empire, by surprise. But not very many days later news came of his grave illness, and in the first month of the new year he died. What his loss meant to his grandchildren, whose greetings, perhaps prophetically, he had given to the children of the Empire in that last broadcast, can be estimated only from the intensity of the grief that was felt even by the millions who had known the King only as a distant public figure. It was the first time that death had struck down one of the Princess's own little world. Queen Mary took her down to Westminster Hall to see the solemn beauty with which a mourning nation surrounded the body of its lost sovereign, as he lay in state. Here was the sadness that dwells in the heart of kingship, for young eyes to blend in one picture, if they could, with the joy and the glory that had been so inspiring in May. A few days later holding her mother's hand in St. George's Chapel, Windsor, the Princess saw her grandfather's body lowered into the grave, and heard Garter King of Arms proclaim the sonorous roll of his titles, followed by an equally magnificent proclamation of those of her uncle David, who was now to be King.

With these mingled memories of sunshine and shadow to reflect upon, the Princess returned to her schoolroom while the momentous year 1936 ran its course. Much happened in that year which portended transformation in the whole character of the world in which Princess Elizabeth and all her generation must live out their lives. Abyssinia was brutally overrun by Italy. The German Army marched into the Rhineland. The guns opened in Spain. And at the end of the year domestic crisis in the Royal Family convulsed the British Empire.

The strange romantic storm of divided loyalties which caused King Edward VIII to renounce the throne of his fathers has nothing directly to do with the life of Princess Elizabeth. It is therefore unnecessary to say anything of the events and motives that brought him to his momentous choice. But the decision he reached had profound consequences for her; and there

was a second choice to be made in which she was vitally concerned. If Edward VIII must cease to be King, it would be necessary for Parliament to amend the Act of Settlement in order to give effect to his decision; and, as the constitutional lawyers who drafted the Bill did not fail to point out, if the Act of Settlement was to be changed it did not follow automatically that the next heir under that Act should succeed King Edward. The new Act must in effect name the new King; and in these unprecedented circumstances it was scarcely possible for Parliament to call any successor to the vacant throne without consulting his personal wishes. It was widely believed that the Duke of York, though himself the most conscientious man in accepting any task, however burdensome, that his duty to the people might lay upon him, was reluctant to sentence his daughters to the lifetime of unremitting service, without hope of retirement even in old age, which is inseparable from the highest place of all. As parents the Duke and Duchess had shown, by the simplicity with which they had brought their children up, what kind of happiness they would most wish them to enjoy. It was certainly seriously considered at this time whether, by agreement among the Royal Family, the crown might not be settled on the Duke of Kent, the only one of the abdicating King's brothers who at that time had a son to become Prince of Wales, and so avoid laying so heavy a future burden upon the shoulders of any woman. The possibility of such a course was debated by some men of authority in the State who believed that it would accord with the wishes of the royal persons concerned. Whether it was ever seriously considered in the royal household itself is of course a matter of which nothing is ever likely to be publicly known. If it became necessary to tender any advice to the Duke of York, it could only have been, first, that his own great reputation for devotion to public service was too universally appreciated for the people to allow him to stand aside, and secondly, that the unpretentious way in which the Princesses had passed their childhood was not only the source of their enormous popularity, but was felt among all ranks and classes of the nation to have provided the ideal early training for a future Queen. In fact, the course actually taken was

DUET—1940

BROADCASTING TO THE CHILDREN OF THE EMPIRE—13th OCTOBER, 1940

merely to remove the present Duke of Windsor and all his descendants from the succession as if he had legally ceased to exist, and to allow the Act of Settlement to take effect as it would normally have done on his death. But a people justly and increasingly grateful for the unwearying service that it receives from the present King and Queen should sometimes pause to recall that they did not take up their heavy burden by any inescapable fate, but might if they so wished have claimed to continue in their less arduous station, and that it was by a free choice that they decided that their daughter owed a duty of her own to their people, which could not for any selfish consideration be put aside.

And so on 12th December, from a window in St. James's Palace, the Princess looked out on a scene of tabarded pomp, and heard the heralds proclaim "That the High and Mighty Prince Albert Frederick Arthur George is now become our only Lawful and Rightful Liege Lord, George the Sixth, by the Grace of God, of Great Britain, Ireland, and the British Dominions beyond the Seas, King, Defender of the Faith, Emperor of India"; and had to realize that this awe-inspiring transformation of her familiar father into a

figure of mystical and emblematic splendour was accompanied by her own promotion to the rank of heir presumptive to the throne. There was no mention of her in the proclamation; but when she went to church on Sunday she would hear herself named in the prayer for the Royal Family and might well feel that, in the formidable prospect now opening out before a small girl not yet turned eleven, she would have need of all the Divine favour that might be granted in response to the petitions of so many millions of Christians throughout the world-wide Empire.

For the next few months preparations for the Coronation dominated the thoughts of the children. Their dresses had indeed been on order for some time, when the Coronation expected was that of their uncle; but now that the solemnity was to be so much more intimately their own family affair, their part would be greater, their robes more splendid, and expectation vastly more exciting.

After the Christmas holidays the family moved into Buckingham Palace, and the home in Piccadilly, where they had spent so many happy years, was dismantled. In the midst of the new magnificence, the Queen, after her wont, set to work to create in their own apartments the quiet homeliness which she and her children loved; and here the dressmakers came and went, while along the Mall outside the carpenters were hammering at their beams and erecting the stands for the multitudes who would assemble on the great day.

When the day came—unhappily it was rather a rainy day—the children had for once to be separated from their father and mother in the celebrations. There is a loneliness inseparable from kingship; and as if to show it the King and Queen had to be isolated in the procession in the majesty of their great crystal coach, where even their children could not accompany them. So the Princesses were placed in the care of their aunt the Princess Royal; and on either side of her they walked to their places in the special gallery which had been erected on the south side of the High Altar at Westminster for the ladies of the Royal Family and their attendants. They had each a long train of purple velvet, and the coronet of a King's daughter ornamented with crosses paty and fleurs-de-lis to put on at the moment when the Archbishop set the crown on their mother's head. But for those of us who looked down from the high galleries on the brilliant scene, all this glory seemed only to accentuate the smallness of the diminutive figures; and one could not but reflect again on the load of responsibility that history was imposing upon shoulders so delicate and frail. It was not possible, however, to indulge such half-melancholy thoughts for long on such a day of universal rejoicing. The august rite moved with stately cadence to its end, and the two Princesses took their places in the procession down the nave, walking together immediately in front of their grandmother Queen Mary; and soon they were coming out on the Palace balcony, still in their robes, to win from the great crowds a special cheer of their own, which seemed even to swell a little louder the mighty acclamation that, before they came, was already saluting the crowned King and Queen.

That was almost the last scene of high pageantry in which Princess Elizabeth would play a part for many a long year; for events were looming ahead in the world which before long would send all the glitter and the colour of life into eclipse. It was the early summer of 1937, the

DRIVING WITH HER SISTER IN WINDSOR GREAT PARK—1941

AT WORK IN HER GARDEN—WINDSOR, 1941

Christmas 1941

PANTOMIME

CINDERELLA

written and produced by H. I. Tannar

Characters

Jemima Blimp	- - -	Anne Crichton
Agatha Blimp	- -	Alathea Fitzalan Howard
Dandine	- - -	Elizabeth Hardinge
Buddy	- - - -	Cyril Woods
Buddy's Aunt	- - - -	Rose Turner
Baron Blimp	- - - -	H. I. Tannar
Cinderella	- -	Princess Margaret Rose
Prince Florizel	- - -	Princess Elizabeth

CHORUS

Band	No. 1 Coy. Training Battalion, Grenadier Guards
Sketch -	Guardsman Fearinside, Guardsman Goodwin
Baritone	- - - Guardsman Godwin
Accordionist	- - - Guardsman Thomas
Quartette	Sergeant Richards, Corporal Cooper, Guardsman Hathaway, Guardsman Biison

WINDSOR CASTLE
19th December, 1941

Rome–Berlin Axis had been founded, and the Nazi leaders were preparing to formulate their first demands upon Czechoslovakia. As yet unaware, like so many much older people, of the bearing of these complicated events in foreign politics upon her own personal life, the Princess turned her back upon the trumpets and standards of the coronation, and returned to the placid routine of Miss Crawford's schoolroom.

By this time she had a full programme of lessons to keep up with. Besides systematic study of the Bible, she was learning both French and Latin. She took up German for a time, but did not pursue it very far. She learned arithmetic and geometry, and, like some others of her sex, discovered that she did not possess much native genius for mathematics. Geography and history already had a substantial place in the curriculum; the latter, owing to the special circumstances of her new position, would some day have to be given predominant importance. English literature took up a good deal of time; and outside the domain of book-learning she was still having lessons in music, dancing, and drawing, for all

MRS. ROOSEVELT AT THE PALACE. *On 23rd October, 1942, Mrs. Roosevelt arrived in London from the U.S.A. after having crossed the Atlantic by air. She was welcomed by the King and Queen, whose guest she was during her stay, and a dinner party was given in her honour. She is seen above with the Royal Family in the Bow Room at Buckingham Palace.*

of which she possessed gifts above the average. It is however one of the native disadvantages of royal birth that no talent of this kind can be developed to any great pitch of intensity; for the one thing that a Queen cannot afford to be is a specialist. It is tempting to speculate what would happen if true artistic genius, with its ruthless claim to dominate personality, were to manifest itself in the heir to a throne. The result would almost certainly be a political disaster and a personal tragedy. Princess Elizabeth, however, would claim no more than a good natural taste in the arts, and a capacity to practise them competently but in moderation. The artistic side of her mind is well-proportioned with her power of learning the more austere subjects, and the innate balance of her personality has been of the greatest assistance in supporting the efforts of those who have endeavoured to make her education a well-rounded introduction to life in all its aspects. For all aspects of life, grave and gay, are alike the concern of modern monarchy.

(II) LIFE IN THE WAR YEARS

THUS, having reached the age of thirteen and a half, Princess Elizabeth was swept, together with all her future subjects, into the uncharted waters of the Second World War. Like everybody else indeed, she found that the early months of the great adventure made unexpectedly little difference to the even tenor of life. She heard her father and his Prime Minister, Mr. Neville Chamberlain, in grave and measured tones, telling the people over the wireless the meaning of the vast and perilous conflict to which they were summoned, and committing the just cause to the providence of God. But then came a pause. The whole country, including little girls of thirteen, had steeled its resolution to withstand immediate and cruel onslaught; but nothing visibly happened. The Princess was at Balmoral when war was declared, and remained for some time at Birkhall on the Balmoral estate ; therefore she was not involved in the operation of dispersing the children from the great cities, of which if she had been at Buckingham Palace she would no doubt have been the representative figure. So at first there was little in the circumstances of war to affect her, except that her teachers began to lay more stress in her lessons on the historical circumstances that had led up to the catastrophe, and that it was speedily decided that she and her sister must be kept out of London for the duration of hostilities. It was not of course realized at that time how long the struggle would last, or that before it ended the Princess herself would be holding her father's commission.

At the New Year then, when the fantastically improbable course of the Anglo-German war had come to a point at which the main public interest was concentrated upon the Russian invasion of Finland, the two Princesses returned from Scotland and went to their old home at Royal Lodge. Sandringham had been closed at the beginning of the war. On 11th May, the day after the Germans marched into Belgium and events suddenly began to flow with the violence of a cataract, the Princesses moved into Windsor Castle, which was to be their residence for the remainder of the war.

Princess Elizabeth was now fourteen; and, in the midst of the epoch-making and terrible days that were crowding upon one another, a new turn was given to her education. It was time to take into serious account the great responsibilities that lay ahead of her, and to deflect her studies in a direction that would prepare her to bear them. She therefore now embarked on the systematic reading of constitutional history, under the direction of a close neighbour of the Castle, Mr. (now Sir Henry) Marten, Provost of Eton, both a highly experienced teacher and a learned writer of historical textbooks.

Constitutional history is not commonly regarded as a school subject. Most pupils who have not been marked out by birth to be in their own persons a part of the constitution, postpone its study until they reach the university. It is however, the very heart and kernel of history, at any rate for those who are looking for a historical approach to the understanding of the world in which they live. It is that aspect of history which turns away from the drama of events and personalities, and tries rather to distil out of the narrative of mortal things the

WARTIME AT WINDSOR. *In 1940 the Princesses went to live at Windsor for the duration of the war. Above, the Princess is seen with her father at stirrup-pump practice in 1941, watched by the Queen and Princess Margaret. Left, Princess Elizabeth sets off on a borrowed bicycle for a ride in the park.*

permanent essence which expresses itself in the institutions that will continue to mould the lives of men and nations through the course of many generations, each of which in turn makes its contribution to their development.

No other country possesses so rich a constitutional history as Great Britain and the British Empire, for no other has remained for so many centuries unaffected by the revolutions that cut a nation off from its past. Everything in England which is most powerful in directing the lives of modern men and women—Parliament, the Church, the Law Courts, the County Organization, the Universities, the City of London and many of the great civic communities—has roots going back to the thirteenth century or before; and oldest of all is the Throne.

It was evidently necessary that the Princess should at least know well the story of the office

of kingship or queenship. But that is not a subject that can be studied in isolation. Through all the centuries the Crown of England has been inseparably welded into the national life, and it has been impossible to attach any meaning to the function of a king except in terms of intimate relation with the functions of a chancellor, a secretary of state, a bishop, a judge, a sheriff, an admiral, a juryman, a member of parliament, a parish constable, and for that matter the agricultural labourer, the housemaid and the factory hand who, as voters, all have their place in the constitution. So it was essential that Princess Elizabeth should read constitutional history as a whole as a necessary part of that fundamental problem of all education, the understanding of herself and her place in the world.

During most of the war the Princess had an hour's instruction from the Provost every week;

HER SIXTEENTH BIRTHDAY. *As Colonel of the Grenadier Guards, the Princess inspects her regiment at a special birthday parade on 21st April, 1942 (above). On the same day she went to the local Labour Exchange at Windsor to register under the youth registration scheme (right).*

SEA RANGER—FEBRUARY, 1943.

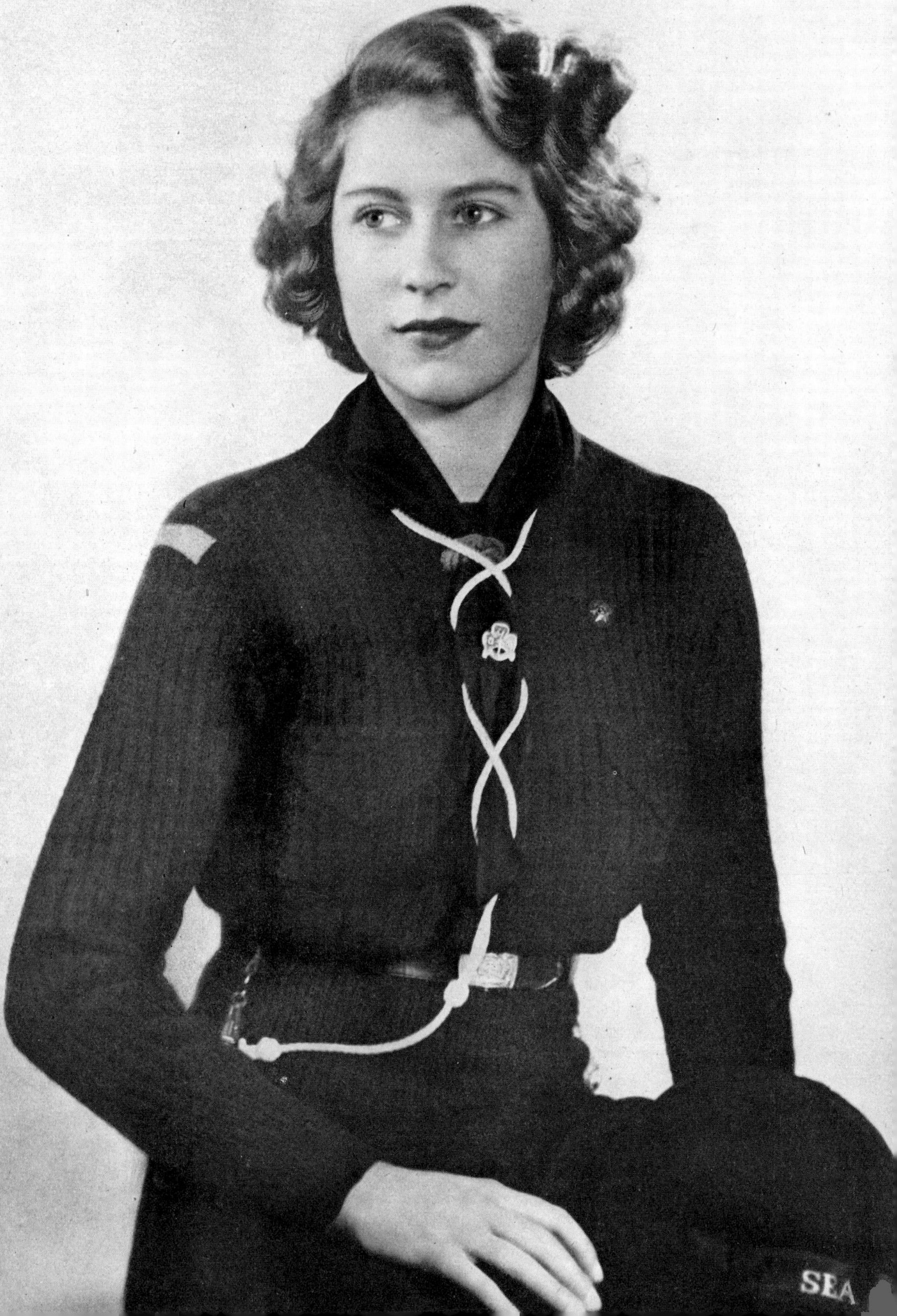

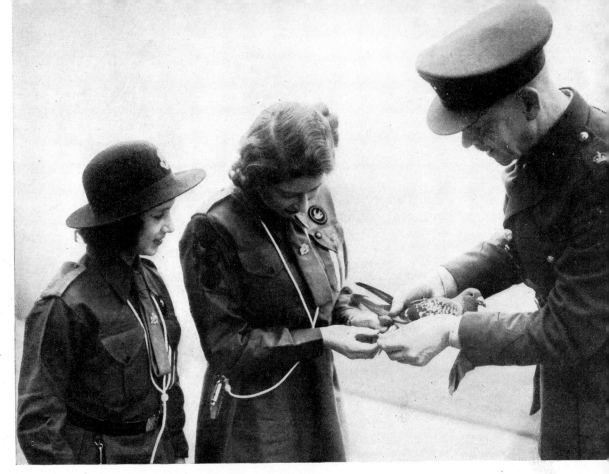

PIGEON POST. *Princess Elizabeth and Princess Margaret Rose, members of the Buckingham Palace Company of Girl Guides, send a message by carrier pigeon to Lady Baden-Powell on 20th February, 1943, which marks the anniversary of the birthdays of the late Lord Baden-Powell and of his wife.*

and, as she began to pass beyond the schoolroom stage of education, he changed the method and gave her twice weekly what was practically a private lecture on constitutional history. Miss Crawford also assisted in the teaching of this vital subject. Gradually lessons merged into a course of study similar to that of an undergraduate in a university; and this continued in spite of the increasing demands of public engagements.

Both Sir Henry Marten and Miss Crawford had taken pains to make their subject as interesting as possible to the pupil, and the books she read as background for her more detailed studies were chosen for the distinction and vividness of the writing as well as for the learning they embody. They included, for instance, Professor Trevelyan's brilliant survey of *English Social History*, with several others of his works, and Lord Elton's book, *Imperial Commonwealth*, in which with profound historical knowledge and real insight into the nature of the imperial ideal he answers the charge that the British Empire is the monument to centuries of greed and aggression, and shows how it has really grown up, by predominantly peaceful means and through the steady spreading of the principles of liberty into backward lands.

History, which with the right treatment can be made a study of the whole of life, was divided by the Provost for Princess Elizabeth's purposes into departments, some of which have been taken up from time to time as subjects for special investigation. One, for example, to which the work of a whole term was devoted, was "The Colonies." Another, which claimed a great deal of time, was "The Evolution of a Self-Governing Dominion." A third was "India and the Indian Problem"; and another group of lectures related to "National Expenditure before the War of 1939" and "National Expenditure during the

War." These last might seem sufficiently austere subjects; but the most elementary student of history soon finds that the whole growth of the parliamentary system and the ideas of liberty and law that it embodies have been conditioned at every stage by considerations of revenue and expenditure.

These headings give an indication of the way in which historical education merged for the Princess into the study of contemporary life. For some years, indeed, time was set aside each week for discussion with the Provost on "Current Affairs." These discussions were for the most part based on newspapers, which the Princess read systematically, often receiving also from Sir Henry a cutting of some article which had caught his own eye and which he asked her to keep for future reference. Tutor and pupil sometimes exchanged letters, the Princess commenting on

HARVEST TIME—1943. *The Royal Family are seen below on a tour of inspection of the harvest at Sandringham. The King and his daughters did their rounds on bicycles whilst the Queen went on ahead with her groom in her pony trap. On the left the Princess is seen with one of the farm horses.*

HIGH SPIRITS. *The Princess has always taken the keenest interest in all the horses in the royal stables. She is seen here with two thoroughbred Norwegian dun ponies, bred by the King at Windsor Castle.*

SOCCER INTERNATIONAL. On 19th February, 1944, Princess Elizabeth accompanied her parents to Wembley to see England play Scotland. Here she is seen with Field Marshal Montgomery watching the game.

BIRTHDAY PORTRAIT—21st APRIL, 1944

From the film " Heir to the Throne."

ANSWERING BIRTHDAY GREETINGS—1944

an article she had read and asking for Sir Henry's opinion. But it was in the weekly meetings that all these ideas about history, as it is passing under the Princess's own eyes, were brought to a focus.

If history leads on into the study of current affairs, so also observation of the life of today must tempt an inquiring mind back into history. A notable example of this arose when the curiosity of the Princess was awakened by operations in Windsor Great Park, part of which was put under the plough in aid of the national campaign to increase the production of food. It lured her into the study of the evolution of English agriculture, and drew from Sir Henry Marten a detailed history of the Windsor farms, specially written for the Princess as an epitome of the agricultural history of the nation.

Education, of course, is not a process of mere reception, but calls for a great deal of creative work on the part of the pupil. The Princess has filled many a notebook or exercise book with her neat and clear writing, which distinctly resembles the Queen's. Much of her work she illustrates with maps, which she draws in pen

and ink and sometimes washes with colour. Her draughtsmanship is easy and elegant, and this geographical side of history, which is dreaded by at least half of the undergraduates who take the highest historical honours at the universities, has always been without terrors for her.

Her exercise books were "marked" by the Provost, fairly and without favour, on the same system that he used for his pupils at Eton.

This sketch of the main staple of the Princess's education, which must be understood as dealing only with the central subject, round which the more usual school lessons in languages, literature, mathematics and the like were grouped, applied in some degree to the general course of her training from the age of fourteen onwards. But in 1940, when its lasting lines were taking shape, it was not possible for any girl of fourteen to concentrate the whole of her mind upon her lessons. In the summer of that terrible year, when France had surrendered and Hitler had announced that the German Army would march into London on 15th September, another heart-searching decision had to be taken by the King and Queen.

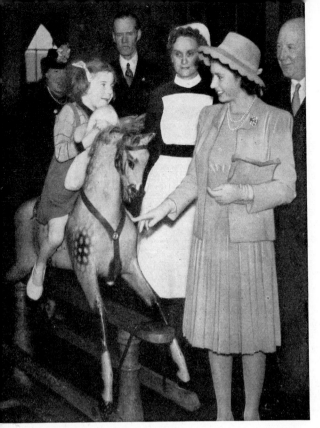

Now that the speeches made by Mr. Churchill in secret session of the House of Commons have been published, there is no room for doubt that those who knew the facts really expected an attempt at invasion to be made, in which at least some German forces would make lodgement upon British soil. This expectation continued even after the Battle of Britain had been won; and when Mr. Churchill in a public speech warned the nation that it might be necessary to plan for a time when the British Isles had been overrun by the enemy, he was not speaking idle words. Therefore, those British parents who decided to save their children from the possibility of a ghastly fate by sending them into the care of hospitable friends in the Dominions and United States were guilty of no hysterical exaggeration of the danger.

No parents were more fully aware of the imminence of the threat than the King and Queen, who knew both the might of the enemy's armament and the desperate scarcity at that time of men, machines and guns with which to oppose it. They had to decide whether their own daughters should be placed in safety, even though they themselves would unhesitatingly remain at their post. The risks were incalculable; and there

were obvious considerations that would make it desirable to have the heir to the throne in a different part of the Empire while the King's life was in jeopardy at home. No one would have ventured to criticize their Majesties if they had allowed this sound constitutional argument to weigh the balance on the side to which their natural feelings as parents inclined; but there were still more weighty considerations on the other side. In that moment of extreme danger it was above all things necessary to sustain public confidence by a resolute, if necessary an ostentatious, display of fearlessness in high places. The children of private persons who had taken refuge across the ocean had no part to play in the defence of the realm, and their departure, far from being an act of desertion, was a strategic advantage to a community under siege. But the Princesses had already begun to become symbolic figures, leaders by birth of the coming generation. The place of leadership is the post of danger; and the

PRESIDENTIAL SPEECH. *On 23rd May, 1944, H.R.H. attended the Annual Meeting of Queen Elizabeth's Hospital for Children in East London, when she made her first independent public appearance. After being elected president, she addressed the meeting (below) and afterwards was conducted round the wards (left) where she talked with the children.*

NAMING AN AMERICAN BOMBER. *The King and Queen, accompanied by Princess Elizabeth and Princess Margaret, visited a bomber station of the 8th U.S.A.A.F. on 6th July, 1944. During the visit H.R.H. christened a new Flying Fortress, "Rose of York," and was presented with a bouquet of white roses by the station commander. Above, she and her parents are seen talking with Lt.-Gen. Doolittle, commander of the 8th Air Force, after the ceremony.*

AT A BOMBER COMMAND STATION. *On 5th July, 1944, the Princess and her parents visited a British bomber station where they met crews who had just returned from an attack on enemy flying bomb bases in France.*

King and Queen, submerging their personal feelings, decided that their children should stay and share all the dangers and privations of the people.

It was, indeed, this episode that gave the occasion for Princess Elizabeth's first public act of leadership. On 13th October, 1940, she delivered a broadcast address in The Children's Hour, in which she spoke to all the children of the Empire and especially to those whom the dangers of the day had separated from their homes. As Mr. McCulloch, the "Uncle Mac" of the B.B.C., has written, the Princess had been rehearsed with scrupulous care by the Queen; and she made a perfect broadcast. After delivering a message of love and good wishes on behalf of all the children at home to those who had gone away she went on:—

> "I can truthfully say to you all that we children at home are full of cheerfulness and courage. We are trying to do all we can to help our gallant sailors, soldiers, and airmen, and we are trying, too, to bear our own share of the danger and sadness of war. We know, everyone of us, that in the end all will be well."

The broadcast ended with an unexpected postscript, when the Princess cried "Come on, Margaret," and Princess Margaret, still only ten years old, added her "Good night, children" to her elder sister's. Mr. McCulloch, who went to Windsor to supervise the broadcast, records how, after the first rehearsal, the King, who had been listening outside, rushed into the room, exclaiming "She is exactly like her!"—meaning the Queen. Thousands of miles away the South African novelist, Sarah Gertrude Millin, wrote in her diary "it was perfectly done. If there are still queens in the world a generation hence, this child will be a good queen."

One other broadcast the Princess made during the war; that was on 30th January, 1945, in a

In the Trench during an alert for flying bombs.
Anne Crichton Ruth Malden, Dawn Simpson, Creina & Muriel Murray Brown, Pat Hobbs, Josephine Burwell Smith, Self, and Iris Woods.
Camp at Frogmore July 1944

HOLIDAY SNAPSHOT.   *A hitherto unpublished photograph taken at Balmoral in August, 1944.   Princess Margaret is on Jock who, as Princess Elizabeth said, was "in a good mood to pose."   H.R.H. has herself written the legends for the pictures which appear on the facing and preceding page.*

Self, Margaret on Hans with Crackers at Balmoral Taken by Roger Hall

From Princess Elizabeth's personal collection.

...s on Jock and Hans... "Balmoral" Taken by ..."crap" Balfour Paul.

very different atmosphere, when General Montgomery's campaign of liberation in Europe was in triumphant career, and she spoke in French a message of thanks to the children of Belgium, whose first act after liberation was to send a collection of their own toys to the nurseries of England. "It is so very hard to part with one's toys," she said. "I know that from experience; but you will believe me when I say that, for that very reason, your presents are all the more valuable to us."

Like other children of her age in that strenuous year, 1940, the Princess, out of school hours, was determined to engage in some sort of activity related to the war effort, and, if possible, in uniform. She chose the Girl Guides. A crew of Sea Rangers was formed, in which daughters of the staff at Buckingham Palace combined with girls from outside who were personal friends of the Princesses. In this crew Princess Elizabeth attained the rank of bosun. She gained several of the badges which are the marks of proficiency among Guides; and when she reached the age of sixteen and was called upon like any other girl to attend for registration at the Windsor Labour Exchange, she wore her Girl Guides' uniform and gave the Girl Guides as her sphere of pre-service training.

For all young people during the war the great dividing line was their eighteenth birthday; for this was the age of calling up. For the Princess, however, it was doubly significant. Had she been called to the throne at any age over eighteen, she would have been competent by law to rule in her own person, and not through a Regent. The possibility of her sudden accession required to be taken very seriously throughout the war years; for it was impossible to ignore the fact that the King, like all his subjects in the British Isles, went in constant danger of his life. Buckingham Palace itself was bombed nine times, from the opening of the Battle of Britain in 1940 to the cessation of the "V" rockets in 1945; and on his frequent visits to the danger points his staff found by experience that the only way to induce him to take cover was to remind him that the crowds who thronged about him would not go to shelter on the sounding of the siren while their King remained exposed. So the senior royal prince in the country, generally the Duke of Gloucester, had to be constantly ready to take

office as Regent on behalf of his niece, in case a sudden disaster had occurred. After 21st April, 1944, that would not have been necessary; indeed, as has been explained in the Introduction, Parliament made her competent to discharge certain other royal functions and she acted several times as a Councillor of State during the King's visits to his forces overseas.

The Bill amending the Regency Act drew particular public attention to the Princess's eighteenth birthday, which was erroneously described in many quarters as her coming of age. Apart from these very special provisions, it was only her calling-up age; but the public functions now beginning to devolve upon her caused the King to announce that these functions, with her continuous training as heiress presumptive, outweighed the claims of ordinary national service. He therefore directed that she should not be called up to any of the auxiliary forces. The Princess herself, however, strongly demurred to this view, and continued to urge its re-consideration. Since the decision was ultimately reversed by its author, it may not be disloyal to express here the opinion that the Princess was right and the King's first thoughts were mistaken. Nothing in the upbringing of the heiress is more important than to ensure that, so far as is humanly possible, she shall share the normal experience of her contemporaries, of whom she is already the representative and will some day be the ruler. That meant, in the circumstances of the war, that she ought to see from the inside one of those auxiliary services which were the characteristic war environment of the girls of her age. After exercising all her persuasion the Princess was allowed to join the A.T.S., and was gazetted to an honorary commission as Second Subaltern in March, 1945.

She was sent at once to join No. 1 Mechanical Transport Training Centre at Aldershot, where she underwent the N.C.O.'s course in the theory and practice of mechanics. The main subjects of this course were: driving of all types of mechanical vehicles, maintenance and service of the same types; night driving; driving in convoy; map reading, and study of the Highway Code. In addition to these branches of the driver's art, the Princess also went through a course in first aid, and was instructed in the various branches of administration that an A.T.S. officer must

From Princess Elizabeth's personal collection.

SHOOTING SEASON AT BALMORAL—1944

understand. These included military law, the regulations for pay and allowances, the routine of clothing issues, and a variety of other topics.

At the time the Princess arrived at Aldershot she had never driven a car and did not even know where the clutch was. So she began her studies with a stationary car on blocks. Under the instruction of her company commander, Junior Commander V. E. M. Wellesley, she then went straight on to the road in a fifteen hundredweight Bedford lorry. Afterwards she was taught to drive a Wolseley staff car, and finally a large field ambulance. These are the three principal types of vehicle that A.T.S. drivers normally handle.

No publicity was given to the Princess's presence at Aldershot, nor was her training allowed in any way to disturb the ordinary routine. At her own request she was treated off parade precisely as any other junior officer; on duty she waived her rank and submitted to the same discipline as the sergeants and corporals who were her fellow pupils. The mornings were devoted to practice on the road and to lectures on mechanics, map reading and the other subjects of the course. In the afternoon there were more lectures, and practical instruction in such necessary jobs as changing wheels and fitting new plugs. It was in this messy employment that Princess Elizabeth, dressed in greasy overalls and with blackened hands, was found by the King and Queen and Princess Margaret when they visited the training centre; and the heir to the throne was able to show them with some pride of achievement, how to put a disabled heavy lorry into working order.

For the world in general this parental visit, which could not be kept secret, brought the first disclosure of where the Princess was and how she was spending her time. At the end of the course Miss Wellesley was able to report that "Her Royal Highness is a very good and extremely considerate driver," and showed the courage of her opinion when she allowed her pupil then and there to drive her from Aldershot to London. The new graduate swept her company commander through the thickest of London's afternoon traffic and into the courtyard of Buckingham Palace; though whether the fact that she found

it necessary to drive twice round Piccadilly Circus on the way was due to high spirits or to a less than absolute mastery of the round-about system has not been determined by competent authority.

From that time the Princess devoted herself to A.T.S. duties with such regularity as the ever increasing pressure of her public functions would allow. She wore her uniform with pride on many ceremonial occasions, and now bears the three stars of a Junior Commander.

Thus for the Princess, as for most other girls of her age, the sterner side of life during the war began with lessons and continued with uniformed public service. The King and Queen saw to it, however, that like other girls their children should enjoy as much of the pleasures of youth as the restrictions and anxieties of the time would allow.

Perhaps a borderline place between business and pleasure may be allowed to A.R.P. training;

LAUNCH OF A NEW BATTLESHIP. *On 30th November, 1944, H.R.H. visited Messrs. John Brown and Company's yard, Clydebank, where she launched Britain's most powerful battleship, H.M.S. "Vanguard." She is here seen passing through a crowd of shipyard workers on her way to the launching ceremony.*

BATHING SCENE. *"Old Mother Red Riding Boots" was the title of the pantomime produced at Windsor Castle at Christmas, 1944. Here Princess Elizabeth is seen emerging from a bathing machine on "Brighton beach" after a "dip." She had previously appeared in a bathing costume of the period.*

for stirrup-pump practice and the like were a family affair, and both parents and children got a good deal of fun out of its inevitable humours. At the same time the harsh realities to which these sports were related did not fail to impinge upon the Princesses' life. It was no secret from them that German bombs were falling upon Buckingham Palace, and that while they remained in comparative safety at Windsor their parents' lives were in danger. They lost also in these years two buildings full of happy memories. One was their childhood home at No. 145 Piccadilly, which was gutted in the raids of 1941. The other was the Bath Club in Dover Street, where they had learned to swim; but this was destroyed by an accidental fire, without, as far as is known, Nazi assistance. Both children had taken to the water very soon after they learned to walk, and both can swim very well. Princess Elizabeth had won the Children's Challenge Shield at the Bath Club only three months before the outbreak of war. After that her regular visits to those baths

perforce came to an end, but she continued to swim at Windsor and elsewhere whenever she had the chance.

All kinds of amusement connected with animals had an irresistible appeal to the Princess. Like the King and Queen, she and her sister have always enjoyed walking in the country; and that almost invariably involved the company of a number of dogs. The two corgis, Crackers and Susan, and the Tibetan lion dog, Ching, have for some time been the reigning favourites.

Riding remained during the war Princess Elizabeth's regular exercise; but although an excellent horsewoman, she has not quite the reckless abandon of Princess Margaret. She has suffered two accidents. As early as December, 1937, when she was not yet twelve, she was thrown by her Shetland pony in the grounds of Sandringham House. She was unhurt, and rode again next day. The second accident, however, was more serious. In September, 1945, she was thrown while riding at Balmoral, and suffered a

PLANTING A RED OAK. *On 3rd March, 1945, the Royal Family planted red oak trees in the form of a cross in Windsor Great Park to commemorate the Red Cross Agricultural War Effort. Princess Elizabeth is here seen planting her tree, assisted by Susan, one of her Welsh corgi dogs.*

bruising of both legs, sufficiently severe to require the attention of the Surgeon Apothecary to the Household and to lead to an announcement in the Court Circular that complete rest for several days had been ordered.

Later on, but not until the war was almost over, the Princess was introduced to the sport of deer-stalking. When she is in Scotland now she is apt to go off all day alone with a ghillie, starting off at nine o'clock in the morning and not coming home until it is nearly dark.

Indoor amusements during the war ranged from mere romps to the serious practice of the Arts. The amiable imbecilities of Animal Grab, Racing Demon, and Old Maid have not even yet lost their hold on the Princess; and she and her sister will go on playing for hours and insist that their elders conform to their taste.

At the other end of the scale the Princess has maintained a lasting enthusiasm for drawing, for music, and perhaps most of all for the theatre. At one time she used to draw and paint her own Christmas cards; although in this accomplishment she would be the first to admit that she falls short of the talent of her younger sister. But her masterpiece in her own particular speciality of lino-cuts need fear no comparison. It was made some years ago as a Christmas card for Queen Mary, and depicted a circus horse of great vivacity.

Music, however, probably means more to the Princess than the visual Arts. She cannot remember a time when it did not play a part in her life; for from nursery days the Duchess of York used to play the piano to her children, and while still very small they would come and stand beside her and sing old Scottish songs and English ballads, even negro spirituals, to her accompaniment. Princess Elizabeth has never given up her pianoforte lessons, and can play the great classical composers as well as the modern dance music which she also enjoys.

The Queen, who herself comes of a musical family, cannot have been surprised to discover that her daughters had a natural taste for music; and she took advantage of their prolonged residence at Windsor to encourage it. She asked Dr. Harris, the organist of St. George's Chapel, to talk to the Princesses about music for a regular period every week. They used to visit him at his house in the Castle Cloisters every Tuesday evening, and hear him tell of the great composers, and of the way their masterpieces took shape. Dr. Harris used to illustrate his remarks on the piano, and sometimes took the Princesses up into the organ loft of the noble Chapel while he played for them. They learned to read a musical score, and even the elements of the conductor's art. With this grounding, Dr. Harris then introduced his pupils to the famous sixteenth-century collection of virginal music known as *Lady Neville's Book*, invoking here the aid of another eminent Windsor character, Dr. Edmund Fellowes, the authority on English madrigal music. So Princess Elizabeth made the acquaintance of William Byrd, the Elizabethan father of all that is most English in musical tradition.

At this stage the Queen intervened again with the suggestion that to make music is even more enjoyable than to listen to it. The result was the inauguration of a series of musical parties, in which the friends of the Princesses were invited to join them in singing part-songs and madrigals. Dr. Harris took charge; some of the choristers of St. George's were soon brought in to reinforce the singers; and soon it became necessary to shift the performances from Dr. Harris's house to the more spacious Red Drawing Room of the Castle. There have been times when V-bombs have forced the singers to take refuge in corners protected from the danger of flying glass; but the musical parties have always gone on. Since the war they have been transferred to the Bow Room at Buckingham Palace, and they are still a regular part of the Princess's life. She and her sister both have true and clear soprano voices, although they have never been formally trained. The choir has an average membership of about twenty-five; and, although they sing for pleasure, they sing seriously and under strict direction by Dr. Harris. The madrigals of their large repertory are sung, of course, unaccompanied. The parties are friendly social occasions, but the only passport to them is a genuine delight in music and willingness to take trouble to make it perfect. There is no audience, except for an occasional visit from the Queen. The motto of the parties might well be the first verse of a famous old English part-song:

> He that hath a pleasant face
>   And will join in catch or glee,
> He shall have a welcome place
>   Mid this goodly company.

TRAINING TO BE AN A.T.S. OFFICER—APRIL, 1945

But the choir would certainly also subscribe to the sentiments of the last verse:—

> If he cannot play or sing,
>   And he only comes to talk,
> Then that's quite another thing:
>   He may take his hat and walk.

Greatly, however, as the Princess enjoys music in all its forms, probably her chief natural talent is for acting. All children, of course, are natural actors; but with her the inborn capacity has continued and developed through the years of adolescence, when in most of us it fades away.

Once again it was the Queen whose insight detected the gift. By way of relieving for her children the anxieties of the most perilous year in modern English history, Her Majesty in 1940 approached Mr. Hubert Tannar, Headmaster of the Royal School at Windsor, with the suggestion that the Princesses might join the pupils at his school, including many who had come from London in the great evacuation, in a little concert. They played piano solos and duets; they also took part in a little scene written by Mr. Tannar for the occasion, called *An Apple for the Teacher*. Princess Elizabeth in cap and gown played the teacher, while four pupils, including Princess Margaret, tap-danced into school. Later on, in a scene in a country inn devised to make a setting for drinking songs, the Princesses were the waitresses who served the drinks.

After the concert had been given at the school, the Queen summoned the company to a "Command Performance" at the Castle; and thus the precedent was set for an annual production, which every Christmas during the war grew more professional and finished.

Mr. Tannar, who has himself provided most of the material for this account of the Princess's stage career, went to dramatic schools as a baby and has been an enthusiastic amateur actor and producer all his life. Being also an accomplished teacher, he was peculiarly qualified to draw out the Princess's theatrical talents. No doubt he did it all the better for the fact, which stands out in every reference he makes to his pupil, that from the beginning, when she was only fourteen, he has been the unresisting victim of her youthful charm. In his eyes, this was the most attractive child he had ever taught.

He was looking, however, especially for the qualities that are useful to a business-like producer, who is solely concerned to make a success of the play. The first such quality, especially when the company are children, was obedience; the child actress must submit herself unresistingly to copy the movements and tones of speech laid down for her by the producer. Princess Elizabeth gave this obedience absolutely and without question; and having thus passed quickly and easily through the rudimentary stage, she was then able to infuse her personality into the theatrical tricks she had first learned by mere imitation. With a quick eye and retentive memory for human character, she soon began to give her parts individuality and life. A strong sense of humour, which is going to serve her well in a world much wider than the stage, has helped her to establish that co-operation between both sides of the footlights which is the secret of dramatic effect.

The first of the Christmas productions was a nativity play called *The Three Roses*, which was given in St. George's Hall at Windsor Castle in 1940. Princess Elizabeth played one of the kings and Princess Margaret a little girl. After the interposition of a dancing and musical show in the summer of 1941, the remaining entertainments were all pantomimes. Princess Elizabeth was generally cast for the part of principal boy, while Princess Margaret "played opposite." They were Prince Florizel and Cinderella in 1941; Prince Salvador and Fairy Thistledown in *The Sleeping Beauty* in 1942; and Aladdin and Princess Roxana in 1943. For the last Christmas of the war a burlesque medley of many pantomimes was put together under the title of *Old Mother Red Riding Boots*; and this time Princess Elizabeth reverted to her own sex as Lady Christine Sharwood, in the height of the fashion of the Edwardian era, as is shown in the photograph on page 89. This costume was a special favourite of the King's; the Princess herself, says the photograph looks as though it came straight out of the family album.

(III) THE BEGINNING OF PUBLIC LIFE

IN July, 1944, King George left England on a visit to his forces in the Mediterranean, and for the first time Princess Elizabeth was appointed a member of the Council of State that exercised the royal functions in his absence, as she was qualified to be by the recent amendment of the Regency Act. She had just passed her eighteenth birthday. Her colleagues in the Council of State were the Queen, the Duke of Gloucester, the Princess Royal, and Lady Southesk, granddaughter of Edward VII, the whole body consisting by law of the Queen and the four adults present in the United Kingdom who stood nearest to the succession.

In the same month the King assigned to his elder daughter armorial bearings consisting of the Royal Arms differenced by a label of cadency —that is, a narrow band with three pendants running across the top of the coat—of silver, with the Tudor Rose on the middle point, and St. George's Cross on each of the others. She displays her arms, according to the heraldic convention for an unmarried lady, not on a shield but on a lozenge.

These formalities were an indication that the heiress presumptive had now become a public figure. She had indeed already emerged from time to time into the light of official or ceremonial activity. Putting aside her broadcast of 1940, which was made on a unique occasion and delivered explicitly as a message from a child to children, she had already performed a public duty on her own account in 1943, before she was seventeen, when she inspected the tank battalion of the Grenadier Guards and took the salute at a march past. The Princess was appointed Colonel of this historic regiment. There is no dignity of which she is more proud; she takes the closest possible interest in the welfare of officers and men of all its battalions, and she misses no opportunity of cultivating their personal acquaintance. She will hereafter become associated with other regiments and corps, and will eventually become the head of the whole army; but it seems probable that the "First Guards" will always remain nearest to her heart.

The year 1944 was full of significant events in the Princess's formal life, each of which was the first of its kind but the precursor of many more that would henceforth make up the routine of her days. These public appearances, it must be remembered, were made against a background of tremendous happenings. Only six weeks after her eighteenth birthday the Allied armies landed

SECOND SUBALTERN IN A.T.S.—1945.

From Princess Elizabeth's personal collection.

ROYAL SNAPSHOT. *A photograph taken by Princess Elizabeth of her parents and her sister with Crackers and Susan at Windsor early in 1945.*

on the Norman shore, and for the next year the majestic sweep of the great campaign of victory dwarfed into insignificance the little incidents of growing up. The Princess undoubtedly felt this herself. Her heart, like everybody else's, was beyond the Channel, where her regiment and many of her personal friends were fighting. But she went through the part allotted to her, with quiet dignity and an increasing assurance, helping now to keep the wheels of life turning at home, and finding wherever she went that a royal visit gave no less genuine pleasure because it was performed, so to speak, in a backwater, while the great currents of history were flowing with such tremendous power elsewhere.

She was much in demand now among all kinds of societies and associations, in which her acceptance of high titular office would imply royal, which is to say national, approbation of the cause for which they worked. This was the occasion for her first official visit alone to the City of London, where she appeared on 31st May, in the Egyptian Hall of the Mansion House, was installed as President of the National Society for the Prevention of Cruelty to Children, and

delivered an able presidential address. In the autumn she made a similar appearance in Edinburgh. On the 23rd September she drove to the Assembly Hall on The Mound and there received on behalf of the Y.M.C.A. the purses containing the money which had been collected for its appeal fund. Thus, both in England and in Scotland her first appearances as the principal figure on a formal occasion were made, as was appropriate, in the cause of youth. It was on a similar occasion that she made her debut in Wales; but that did not take place till the following year. On 2nd June, 1945, she attended the council meeting of the Girl Guides at Cardiff and made a speech to an audience of over four thousand people. This was not, however, her first visit to Wales. She had made a tour of the country with her parents in March, 1944; and she has always taken a special interest in the Principality from which, if she had been born of the other sex, she would have derived her highest title.

The year 1944 also saw the beginning of the Princess's social career. The evening courts, at which in time of peace debutantes of her age would normally be presented to their Sovereign,

were still suspended; otherwise no doubt the Princess would have been a brilliant figure in the proceedings. Perhaps the nearest approach to a "coming out" that she enjoyed was her first appearance at a big dinner party on 1st May, 1944. There could not have been a more auspicious occasion, for the party was given by the King and Queen at Buckingham Palace in honour of the Dominion Prime Ministers who were in London at the time. Unhappily, it had not been found possible to bring together a complete muster of the five heads of governments; indeed, no such meeting has assembled since the Coronation year. But the Princess sat between General Smuts, Prime Minister of the Union of South Africa, and Mr. Mackenzie King, Prime Minister

THANKSGIVING SERVICE. *On the first Sunday after VE-Day, 13th May, 1945, the Royal Family attended a Thanksgiving Service in St. Paul's Cathedral. Here they are seen being received by the Dean of St. Paul's on their arrival.*

the Commonwealth, even though in due time her constitutional advisers will inevitably be men of a much younger generation than these two famous veterans. Since that evening the Princess has rapidly extended her personal friendships among men and women of high authority in public affairs. She always shows herself modestly appreciative of the opportunities that come to her for direct intercourse with the leading minds of the day. She can talk well herself, but on these occasions she shows herself primarily as the perfect listener, storing away in a retentive memory the ideas and the wisdom that come to her from the lips of men of such great experience.

Some of the important ceremonial events in which the Princess took part during this year of growing up had still to be concealed from public knowledge owing to the wartime necessities of security. Nothing, for instance, could be said of the visit of the whole Royal Family on 29th October to H.M.S. *King George V*, lying at Greenock; and still less was it possible to mention that on 30th November Her Royal Highness herself took the leading part on a great naval occasion. On that day she went to the famous shipyard of John Brown & Co. on Clydebank, and there launched the battleship *Vanguard*, which in 1946 was the most powerful capital ship in the world. Her banner of arms, popularly called her personal standard, was this day broken for the first time from the flagstaff in the shipyard. The Princess played her part unfalteringly, smashing the traditional bottle of wine upon the steel prow as the hull slipped away towards the water, and in clear accents praying for good luck to the ship and all who should sail in her. One of these, as it has turned out, is Princess Elizabeth herself; for the unexpectedly rapid collapse of all the King's enemies in 1945 postponed, it is to be hoped for ever, the necessity for the great ship to fire her guns in battle, and, in fact, the first important service assigned her was to carry the King, with his family, on the state visit to his subjects in the Union of South Africa.

of the Dominion of Canada. The juxtaposition of the future head of the Empire with the two longest established of its elder statesmen was a striking and emblematic event. It was also significant for the Princess's education; for it is of the first importance in her training for the place that she will one day fill that she should make the personal acquaintance of all the eminent men of

Busy, however, as the Princess was in 1944 with public and semi-public ceremonies, with visits to

FAREWELL TO CIVIL DEFENCE. *The Queen and Princess Elizabeth admiring Peter, a member of one of the canine rescue squads, during the stand-down parade of Civil Defence Services in Hyde Park on 10th June, 1945.*

IN NORTHERN IRELAND. *On 17th July, 1945, the Princess left England with her parents on a tour of Northern Ireland. She is seen here in conversation with a Brownie during an inspection of Girl Guides at Londonderry.*

the troops, with social appearances at the opera and the Windsor Horse Show, where both she and her sister won prizes, this year represents rather the overture than the first act of her public life. The interval was filled by her training in the A.T.S., which has already been described; and it was not till her emergence in the summer of 1945 from the strenuous routine of Aldershot that she was able fully and finally to take her place as a public personage.

In a sense she moved into her place in the main stream of the national life as the daughter of victory. She was just nineteen when the Germans surrendered; and when on the evening of VE-Day she appeared in uniform with her parents and sister on the balcony at Buckingham Palace, the many thousands who cheered were perhaps conscious for the first time of her significance as an emblematic figure of the future, of all for which the nation had fought and suffered and of the hopes of a better world for their children to inherit. Eight times in the course of that evening the Royal Family appeared on the balcony, and it was not till twenty minutes after midnight that the windows were closed for the last time and the Princess could go to bed with her memories of the great struggle which had closed her childhood and moulded the world in which her adult life would be lived.

In the following week she shared with the King and Queen in their two Victory tours of London, on the north side of the river on 9th May and on the south side on the tenth; and on the Sunday the whole Royal Family drove to St. Paul's to render thanks to God on behalf of all their people. On 16th May they journeyed to Edinburgh to take part in a similar thanksgiving in St. Giles's Church; and next day they were back in the Palace of Westminster, where the Queen and the Princesses sat beside the King in the Royal Gallery while the Lord Chancellor and the Speaker, in their state robes embroidered with cloth of gold, presented loyal addresses of congratulations from the two Houses of Parliament.

In August the whole series of celebrations and observances was repeated, this time with more profound and final significance because the guns had fallen silent at last all over the world, though perhaps not with quite so tremendous a relief of tension as had followed the collapse of the first and principal enemy. The formal proceedings in both London and Edinburgh were very much the same as before; but something new was added to the rejoicings round Buckingham Palace when the two Princesses left their parents to take the salute from the balcony and themselves went down, escorted by officers of the Brigade of Guards, to move among the cheering crowds below. It was a most popular gesture, and gave deep pleasure to all those in the great multitude who were fortunate enough to be close to the lanes that opened up wherever the little party moved.

Since the end of hostilities, the Princess's engagement list has become almost as crowded as those of the King and Queen. Although she continued to live at home, it had become necessary even in 1944 to begin the formation of what is technically called "a household" for her, whose members might both accompany her on her public appearances and cope with the secretarial work that was beginning to mount up behind the scenes. The first to join her as lady in waiting was Lady Mary Strachey, wife of Lord O'Hagan's heir, Captain Thomas Strachey, and youngest daughter of Lord Selborne. This was on 11th July, 1944. In March, 1945, her increasing duties began to be shared with the daughter of Mr. A. V. Hambro, of Milton Abbas, the widowed Mrs. Vicary Gibbs, who on 29th May, 1946, became the wife of the Queen's nephew, the Hon. Andrew Elphinstone. Princess Elizabeth was one of the bridesmaids at the wedding, and after the honeymoon Mrs. Elphinstone resumed her functions in the household. Meanwhile, on 20th May, a third lady in waiting had been appointed in the person of Lady Margaret Egerton, Lord Ellesmere's daughter, to whom it fell to attend the Princess on the present visit to South Africa. All three ladies are in the middle twenties, for the members of the Princess's staff are intended to be friends and companions, and it is desirable that they should be close to her in age.

The lady in waiting who is for the time being in attendance acts as the Princess's private secretary, having taken over that function from the Queen's ladies, who used to deal with the heavy correspondence that was addressed to Princess Elizabeth even as a child. The lady in waiting takes the Princess her letters in the morning, and receives her instructions about how they are to be

A SMILE FOR BABY. A picture taken during a visit to the Heritage Craft Schools for Crippled Children at Chailey, Sussex, on 27th June, 1945.

WITH THE SEA RANGERS. Learning to sail on Virginia Water whilst in camp with the Sea Rangers in July, 1945.
From Princess Elizabeth's personal collection.

answered. But Princess Elizabeth writes her personal letters with her own hand, and is always specially punctilious in writing letters of thanks herself, when she has accepted any kind of hospitality.

The crowded and miscellaneous programme of engagements which now rules the Princess's life serves several important purposes: it enables her to see a great deal of the country and a great variety of people in their characteristic environments of work or play; it multiplies the number of men and women who have had a sight of and perhaps a personal contact with their future Sovereign; and it enables the encouragement of royal patronage to be given to many worthy enterprises. The Princess would, no doubt, like to be able to say that no good cause that applied for her formal patronage was ever refused. That is impossible, for she has only 365 days in her year, and a glance at her engagement book would show how desperately overcrowded they already are. But the selection of public and other bodies to be visited is made with the utmost care to make it representative of all that is most admirable in the life of the nation, and with far more attention to popular wishes than to the convenience of the Princess herself.

Her Royal Highness finds it particularly difficult to withhold her personal association from any cause charged with the care of the sick; and especially she interests herself in suffering children. She is, for instance, President of the Queen Elizabeth Hospital for Children at Hackney, and also of the Queen Elizabeth League for Children. As has already been said, her first ceremonial appearance in the City of London was as President of the National Society for the Prevention of Cruelty to Children. In addition she is President of the Prince of Wales General Hospital, of the Cardiff Royal Infirmary, and of the Student Nurses' Association of the Royal College of Nursing; and she is Patron of the Red Cross Societies of both Australia and Canada.

Her interest in her own regiment is reflected in her acceptance of the appointment of Patron of the Guards Girls' School; and an association of her own childhood was continued when she became Commodore of the Sea Rangers. She has, however, a wider interest in all matters that concern youth and education, particularly when they are connected with the Services. She is President of the Royal Schools for the Daughters of Naval and Marine Officers, Patron of the Royal Navy and Marines' Home at Chatham, Vice-Patron of the Royal Albert School; while as Vice-Patron of the Life Saving Society she lends her name to what is really another and very valuable branch of education.

The Princess's undiminished delight in animals is acknowledged by her position as Patron of the Welsh Pony and Cob Society; and she attaches much more than ceremonial value to the compliments that have been paid her in the realm of music. She is President of the Royal Amateur Orchestral Society; and the Royal College of Music, in making her their President, were proud to welcome a practising devotee of the art, who even today manages to fit in a weekly piano lesson from Miss Mabel Lander, who has been her tutor since she was four years old.

These honorary offices and dignities, of which the bestowal is an act of loyalty on the part of the bodies that make it, and the acceptance by the Princess is a certificate of their worthy place in the national life, are only the beginning of a list that will grow longer and longer as her years increase. Such appointments are themselves only a small part of the recognition she gives in her representative capacity to many and varied public activities. Wherever she goes she carries by her mere presence a message of encouragement to some group of men and women, or boys and girls, whose corporate activity, however specialized, is by the Princess's visit drawn into contact with all the rest of the multifarious life of the people. Sometimes—indeed now very frequently —this message is delivered in the form of an actual speech; and many audiences have discovered that the Princess, whose voice is clear and beautifully modulated, is capable of speaking straight to the hearts of hearers widely separated by interest and character, with the same directness that they have long known in her mother. Of course, these speeches are not generally of Her Royal Highness's personal composition. She cannot be expected to have the detailed knowledge of each audience she addresses that would enable her to speak *ex tempore* about the particular activity or purpose that has brought them together. Information as a rule has to be sought from the society itself, on which a draft speech can be prepared by the Princess's personal staff. But she

herself studies and criticizes the draft with close attention; she makes her own amendments; and by the time it is ready to be delivered the speech has always taken the impress of her personality. On at least one occasion she has shown that the preparatory work of her assistants is an aid rather than a necessity; for once when she was about to deliver a speech at Windsor a gust of wind carried her manuscript away. There was con-sternation, and a hasty attempt to send for the carbon copy; but the Princess calmly waved her rescuers aside, and delivered an admirable little speech out of her head.

Only a few specimens of the kind of functions, with or without speeches, that Princess Elizabeth attends need be given here. They are familiar to all readers of the newspapers, although it is only by looking at the continuous list of her engage-

PASSING-OUT PARADE. Princess Elizabeth took the salute and presented belts of honour at a passing-out parade at Sandhurst on 27th October, 1945. Here she is seen walking between lines of tanks during her inspection.

ments, as tabulated for a period of a month or so, that one can appreciate how much energy and versatility are demanded of her. A great many of these engagements fall to the Princess in connexion with the fighting Services, who are entitled to regard her since she received her commission as, so to speak, one of themselves; and the royal compliments that she thus pays them acquire thereby a rather different tone and emphasis from those appropriate to the King in whose name they serve. Most solemn and significant of these observances was her appearance on 11th November, 1945, the last Armistice Day under the old ritual, to lay a wreath for her own generation at the foot of the cenotaph in Whitehall. She makes an increasing number of formal inspections, particularly of her own Grenadier Guards, but also of other units of all three

Services. Of special interest among such engagements may be quoted her inspection of Number 1 Mechanical Transport Training Centre, Camberley, in which she herself had received her training (3rd August, 1945); a presentation of belts of honour at the passing-out parade at Sandhurst (27th October, 1945); the review of the Army Cadet Force in Hyde Park (7th April, 1946), at which she took the salute; a visit to Greenock, on 12th May, 1946, to attend the commissioning service on board H.M.S. *Vanguard*; and her attendance with the King and Queen (14th July, 1946) at a simple service held in the churchyard of St. Mary's, Great Bircham, when His Majesty unveiled the Cross of Sacrifice that the Imperial War Graves Commission had erected in memory of the airmen who are buried there.

Naturally the women's Services appear frequently on the Princess's programme. She attended the passing-out parade of A.T.S. Cadets at the Imperial Service College, Windsor, on 13th June, 1946; was entertained at the Ex-Service Women's Club in Edinburgh on the twenty-eighth of the same month; saw the parade of airwomen of the Royal Canadian Air Force on 23rd October, 1945. She took the salute at a march past of the Women's Land Army at Bedford (14th February, 1946), and at a similar celebration of the Rangers in Hyde Park (19th May, 1946), and attended a rally of the Girls' Training Corps a week later, making speeches on all three occasions.

Perhaps the most important public function that Princess Elizabeth has yet discharged separately from the King and Queen is her visit to Northern Ireland, which lasted from 18th to 21st March, 1946. She travelled with the naval state proper to an heir to the throne, in the cruiser H.M.S. *Superb*, which hoisted her personal banner for the occasion. In the course of the visit she launched the then largest aircraft carrier in the world, H.M.S. *Eagle*, and made a speech at the luncheon afterwards, in which she paid royal tribute both to the ancient craftsmanship of the British shipbuilding industry and to the prowess of the Fleet Air Arm, especially as exhibited by the men of that other *Eagle* which was sunk in the Mediterranean in August, 1942. To an island race with centuries of seafaring tradition in their blood, she said, there was something deeply

moving in the launching of a ship, which could not be understood by the peoples of those countries to whom the sea was only of secondary importance. To anyone with a feeling for English history it must have been equally moving to hear a royal Elizabeth speaking to them of the meaning of sea power. Such a repetition of history, in the words Her Royal Highness used of the naval tradition, "is something so very much our own."

After this ceremony, which was the central purpose of the visit, the Princess made a tour of two hundred miles through the counties of Tyrone, Fermanagh and Armagh, visited Dungannon High School for Girls, made another speech at Enniskillen, inspected the Royal Ulster Constabulary, who explained to her the working of an illicit still, inspected a guard of honour at Armagh, and still found time to pay a personal courtesy by standing as godmother at the christening of the baby daughter of Lieut.-Commander Osborne-King. Everywhere she went in her swift progress she was received with unbounded enthusiasm; and the visit was remembered as a truly royal acknowledgment of all that Ulster had done to speed the victory of the British Commonwealth in the Second World War.

A few months after this visit, full as it was of martial symbolism, the Princess was the central figure in a ritual whose whole emphasis lay upon the arts of peace. It is the ancient rule of the Gorsedd of the Bards of Wales that no Bard may bear a naked weapon against or in the presence of anyone, and no one is permitted to do so in their presence, "for a Bard is the minister of peace, refuge and justice." To this immemorial fellowship Princess Elizabeth was admitted on 6th August, 1946, according to the ceremonial contained in *Meyrg of Glamorgan's book*; and she herself declared the Eisteddfod open, wishing all blessings to Wales with the words: "*Rwyf yu agor yr Eisteddfod a phob bendith i Gymrn.*" On the hilltop of Mountain Ash, Glamorgan, she was called within the Circle of Refuge of the Gorsedd wearing the green robe of an Ovate, which is symbolic of "the growth and increase of learning and genius." There the Arch-Druid, standing before the Logan Stone, took her two hands in his and said in Welsh:

"In the name of the Gorsedd of Bards of the Isle of Britain and the National Eisteddfod of Wales"

ROYAL SISTERS—1946

LAUNCHING H.M.S. *EAGLE*—19th MARCH, 1946

BEHIND THE SCENES AT THE CIRCUS—APRIL, 1946

bade welcome to Elizabeth of Windsor. A fanfare of trumpets went echoing round the hills, and the sword-bearer saluted the new Bard by raising aloft the sheathed sword of peace; and then after a short benediction, spoken in English, the great crowds gathered outside the circle of stones and closed the ceremony by singing, in the perfect harmony that only a Welsh assembly can achieve, the venerable anthem of the Principality, "*Hen Wlad fy Nhadau*," or "Land of my Fathers."

Thus Princess Elizabeth, like her parents before her, associated herself with that passionate devotion to the ancient tradition of poetry, music and song which is the heart of Welsh patriotism. There have been times in the long course of history when Wales has thought, not without reason, that the English crown cherished the desire to obliterate the individuality of this small, proud people. Some of the most venerated names in Welsh history have been the names of leaders of revolt. But these unhappy memories serve only to illuminate the changed relation between the two races in modern times. As in the wider ambit of the whole British Commonwealth,

so within the older and closer association of the British Isles, the imperial policy of today is always to preserve, stimulate, and develop what is best in the native tradition of the smaller peoples, in the belief that in freedom and variety, rather than in an imposed uniformity, resides the strength and even the unity of the whole. It is in maintaining this unity in diversity that the Royal Family, who alone in the British Commonwealth have no exclusive association with any one of its component parts, render one of their characteristic and most valuable services.

It would be tedious to catalogue the many ceremonial or public appearances of Princess Elizabeth from the time when she emerged upon the stage of national affairs. Each of them is remembered as a red-letter day in the life of some town or village, some association or community or industrial firm. Each of them for a moment lifted one of these little groups into the light of national interest, and made of its activities a subject to be read about in the newspapers. It is for the health of every part of a great nation that it should take its turn to be the centre of the

THE EAST END GREETS THE PRINCESS—MAY, 1946.

H.M.S. *VANGUARD* COMMISSIONED. *On 12th May, 1946, H.R.H.*
visited Greenock to attend the commissioning of H.M.S. "Vanguard." She was
received by Captain W. G. Agnew, C.B., C.V.O., D.S.O., commander of the
ship (above). On right she is seen leaving the battleship after the service.

attention of the whole. A royal visit gives it that opportunity. But to recapitulate the record of Princess Elizabeth's crowded days would largely defeat the object of her labours; for her royal courtesies, of which the separate significance of each depended upon singling out some particular community for honour, would necessarily lose that significance by throwing them all together once more in the dead level of a list.

The list, however, is always there, a steady programme of duty to be conscientiously worked through, as a background to any recreation that the Princess is able to enjoy. The evident danger for any girl who is thrown almost straight from the schoolroom into such an endless round of public activities is that her whole life may be swallowed up in formal routine, and she may grow old before her time. The King and Queen have always been rightly determined that their children shall enjoy as many as possible of the natural pleasures of youth, and

keep the freshness and gaiety which should be the birthright of the whole people, and which they, far more than their elders in the Royal Family, have a natural mission to represent. In the first years of recovery from the drabness and austerity of war, it has been a real contribution to the brightening of the atmosphere that the heiress to the throne should begin to be seen more and more in all kinds of lighter-hearted activity. No doubt, when she goes to a dance or a concert or a race-meeting, she is seeking amusement and relaxation, without any kind of ulterior motive. It is nevertheless true that by taking an unstudied part in these normal entertainments of daily life, she helps to spread through all ranks of society the right and proper doctrine that, even or especially at a time when a great effort is being demanded of all, the graces and pleasure of life are as essential to the general health as its labours.

So it is natural that in these years since the war the Princess has come to be seen fairly frequently

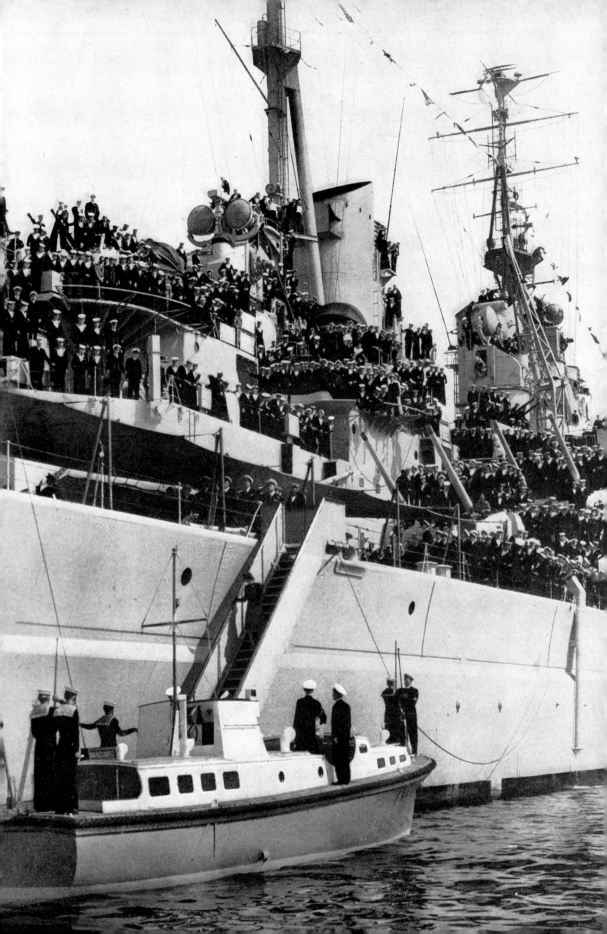

EPSOM RACES

DERBY DAY, 1946

at dances, theatres and concerts, and on many sporting occasions out of doors. Even these hours of pleasure, however, are very frequently combined with indirect service to good causes. She attends many charity performances at the theatre; and if she goes to a big ball it is as likely as not to be given in aid of some deserving fund. She has been a good dancer since her childhood, and now manifestly gets the same endless amusement out of it as the many young girls in every rank for whom it is the central feature of social existence. She dances with tireless energy. Shy young men who are apt to be overawed at the idea of dancing with a Princess soon find in her a cheerful and unassuming companion who is out to enjoy herself on equal terms with them. Her cultivated taste in classical music does not prevent her from sharing the popular enthusiasm for the rhythms of the dance-band leaders whom the twentieth century has raised to such a singular eminence in public esteem.

The theatre gives the Princess the pleasure that would naturally be expected in one who has herself devoted so much of her time to amateur acting. She has sometimes broken away from the rigid convention that royal personages must always be secluded in a box and has from time to time been seen sitting among the audience in the dress circle or the stalls. Her taste is catholic, with perhaps a slight leaning to shows of the lighter sort; but the notable performances that she has seen include one of the *Œdipus Tyrannus* given for charity at the New Theatre in April, 1946, and the productions of the Comédie Française Company at the same theatre in July, 1945. In musical drama she enjoys both grand opera and Gilbert and Sullivan; and she took care not to miss the re-opening of Covent Garden with a season of ballet on 20th February, 1946.

Among outdoor entertainments, although she has watched most kinds of sport, including such outstanding events as Test matches and international football, the Princess's favourite is undoubtedly racing. She has been on intimate terms with horses all her life and understands the finer points of the sport. She goes to the Derby and Ascot

ROYAL WINDSOR HORSE SHOW—JUNE, 1946. *H.R.H. enjoys a joke with some of the judges during her visit to the horse show.*

ROYAL ASCOT—JUNE, 1946. *The King and Princess Elizabeth watching the racing from the roof of the stand on the opening day of the meeting.*

in royal state, and attends a good many smaller meetings informally. She generally likes to have a financial interest in a horse she favours, but confines her betting to merely nominal amounts. It may be confidently expected that she will hereafter take a close and informed interest in the royal stud and in the fortunes of the King's colours on the turf.

So in an ever more strenuous routine of work and play Princess Elizabeth approaches her twenty-first birthday. Behind the crowded record of the things she does there has been slowly taking shape all the time the thing she is. The character that has formed itself, or been shaped by events, through these twenty-one years of childhood and adolescence, will in time to come be one of the influences that will shape history. Its lines, nevertheless, are still very lightly engraved. It will be for life to deepen them, add to them, and perhaps turn them in new directions. Throughout the Princess's education everything has been done to prevent her ideas from becoming too soon fixed or rigid; and she comes to maturity with an open mind. This is her first qualification for her future part as head of a great empire, of which as yet she has seen only one corner. She has all her most vital experience still to gain; she is still able to approach it with all the freshness and flexibility of youth.

The Princess is, therefore, above all, a learner. (Characteristically, on receiving the invitation to South Africa, she sat down to the study of Afrikaans.) She may well remain so all her life, for she is to be the representative of a nation that will constantly change as it travels through the changing years, and she must keep her own mind sensitive to its growth and receptive to all its thoughts and new interests. But her power of reception will not in later years be so great as it is today. At present she is eagerly open to all fresh ideas and experiences, and she stores them away in the keeping of an accurate memory and an orderly mind. They will fill out and develop the contour of her personality as she grows older, but they also take the colour of her mind as it already is.

Some hints of Princess Elizabeth's general outlook on life, to which all her new impressions have to be adapted, may be inferred from the indications of her special tastes and interests which have been given in the foregoing pages. Something more, perhaps, may be derived from a glance at her well-filled book shelves; for it is in the reader's armchair that study and relaxation, the grave and the gay, come most easily together and blend to make one of the characteristic ingredients of an individual mind; a literary facet of a personality.

On the more solid side of the Princess's collection of books one is struck at once by the prominence of history—of history which is also great literature. There will be found the majestic irony

VICTORY SALUTE. Field Marshal Montgomery driving past the Royal Stand during the Victory Parade in London on 8th June, 1946.

BACHELOR OF MUSIC. *On 10th July, 1946, H.R.H. received the honorary degree of Bachelor of Music at the London University. Above, the Chancellor, the Earl of Athlone, admits his great-niece to the degree.*

of Gibbon's *Decline and Fall of the Roman Empire*; the glittering rhetoric of Macaulay's *History of England*; the melodious persuasion of Froude's *Queen Elizabeth*, the contorted declamation of Carlyle's *History of the French Revolution*, and the strategic deployment of the great forces of history which fills the four volumes of Mr. Churchill's *Life of the Duke of Marlborough*. With these great voices sounding in her ears the Princess may claim to have experienced the whole sonorous range of the music of English prose. But although these books are great literature, there is also a scientific side to historical study; and all who embark upon it eventually awake to the realization that there is ultimately no history except the original authorities. To be a real historical student and not a dilettante is to have passed that turning point; and the evidence that Princess Elizabeth has passed it is to be found in her well-used copies of such collections of contemporary

documents as the Letters of George III and George IV.

These witnesses to the diligence of the Princess as a student may be balanced by others that suggest that she does not read history merely as a task. She loves also its colour and romance, and is a voracious reader of historical novels, both those of the older masters, and the examples of a newer technique by such modern writers as Miss Margaret Irwin.

This knowledge and enjoyment of history cannot fail to have developed in the Princess the historian's characteristic vision of life as one organic drama, in which no event is without its continuing repercussions through the ages, and no happening of today can be understood without knowledge of all that went before. "All our past acclaims our future," says Swinburne, and that sense of having a place in a proud succession is a central element in the Princess's mind. It would

RELAXATION—1946. *The Princess is frequently seen at dances and theatres. Above, at the Royal Caledonian Ball in London, she is enjoying a Scottish reel; below, she is seen at the first night of "La Boheme" at the Cambridge Theatre.*

PORTRAIT IN EVENING DRESS—1946

IN THE MUSIC ROOM AT BUCKINGHAM PALACE—1946

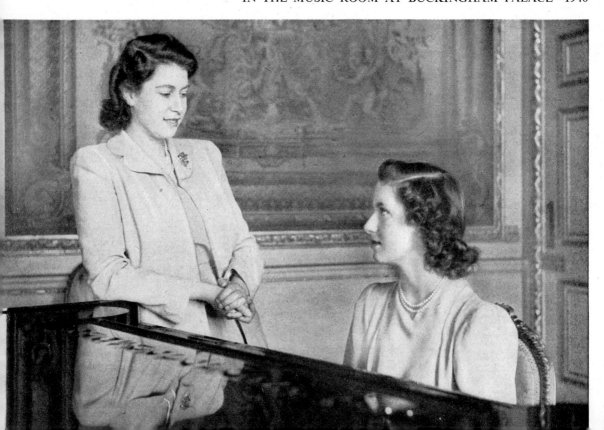

THE NEW BARD. *On 6th August, 1946, H.R.H. attended the National Eisteddfod of Wales, at Mountain Ash, when she was admitted to the circle of the Bards of Wales. Here, standing before the Logan Stone, wearing the robe of an Ovate, she is being received into the Order by the Arch-Druid.*

GUESTS AT BALMORAL. *General of the Army Eisenhower, his wife and son were guests of the Royal Family in October, 1946.*

be so even if she only inherited, in the same anonymous way that we all do, the great legacy of British history; but evidently the appeal of the story is redoubled for a girl who finds the pages crowded with names of her own ancestors and friends. Princess Elizabeth has been fascinated by the figure of her great-great-grandmother, Queen Victoria, and has read a great deal about her. She knows well Lytton Strachey's famous biography, and the affectionately humorous little plays of Laurence Housman; but here also she is in a position to check modern reinterpretations by reference to the authorities, for she is familiar with the big red volumes of the Queen's massive correspondence, and also with her *Leaves from the journal of our life in the Highlands*. The latter work, which enabled the courtly Disraeli to say to the Queen "We authors, Ma'am," may not rank high as literature, but is a uniquely valuable key to the understanding of its author's mind; and from the Princess's point of view it has the charm of showing, under the light of another century, the scenes round Balmoral that she herself loves.

Turning from the shelves that stand for education merging into life, one cannot help being struck by the prominence in the Princess's glass-fronted book cases of the books that represent her life-long interest in animals, and particularly in horses. Anna Sewell's *Black Beauty*, which was her favourite book almost since she

could first read, has been re-read many times since, and even now still keeps its place. It has been joined with the passing of the years by many other books about horses. Such tastes are perhaps shared by most children, who generally seem to find that animals make more exciting characters in fiction than their own species. But with Princess Elizabeth the taste has continued into adult life, and there are few recent books of note about horses or dogs that she has failed to acquire. They range from romantic fiction, in Miss Enid Bagnold's *National Velvet*, through art in Sir Alfred Munnings's collection, *Pictures of Horses and English Life*, and sporting history in Mr. R. C. Lyle's *Royal Newmarket* to the borders of scientific zoology in Dr. Julian Huxley's *Animal Language*. This pleasantly simple perpetuation of a juvenile taste does not preclude a considerable knowledge of classical English literature. The Princess has read all the major plays of Shakespeare; but with this exception her natural taste runs mainly to the works of nineteenth-century authors. Her favourite poets include Shelley, Byron and Wordsworth, and in the next generation Tennyson and Browning. In prose her preference leans towards the more delicate and subtle writers, and away from the robust humours of the Victorian age. Thus she is fond of Jane Austen, and in a more intense vein of the Brontës; but in common with a large section of her generation she has never acquired much liking for Dickens. Among writers of the present day she has a catholic taste, enjoying the adventure stories of John Buchan, the irony of Mr. E. M. Forster, the social satire of H. G. Wells and the ingenious puzzles of Miss Dorothy Sayers. Long family histories, however, of the kind most notably represented by Galsworthy's *Forsyte Saga*, are not to her taste. Books about the sea have a special appeal to her: recent novels like those of Mr. C. S. Forester, famous books of the last century like *Mr. Midshipman Easy*, and Dr. John Masefield's *A Sailor's Garland*, which was her eighteenth birthday present from the crew of the Sea Ranger ship, *President III*, in which she holds the responsible position of bosun. She also enjoys the frivolities of Miss Angela Thirkell.

The Princess reads French almost as easily as English, and has a large collection of French books. She finds French poetry over-sentimental for her taste but enjoys Balzac, Daudet, Anatole France and other great masters of prose. The plays she saw when the Comédie Française came to London in 1945 were Molière's *L'Impromptu de Versailles* and Beaumarchais' *Le Barbier de Seville*.

This reading is supplemented by a painstaking study of the newspapers; and for some time the Princess has been receiving Hansard's Parliamentary Debates. The books she reads are for the most part of her individual choice, which is mainly guided by the reviews in weekly and other papers.

The taste indicated by this selection of literature is that which is natural to a well-trained, active, but still very youthful mind. There is nothing forced about it, nor is there any highly specialized leaning, beyond that which proceeds from the particular bias that has been given deliberately to the Princess's education. Princess Elizabeth reads as most of us do for three equally good reasons: first to amuse herself, secondly to equip herself for the responsibilities she will have to bear, and thirdly to satisfy her curiosity about the world.

All this, then, serves to accentuate the prevailing feature of Princess Elizabeth's character, which is simplicity and naturalness. She has been

ROYAL BRIDESMAIDS. *At the wedding of Lady Patricia Mountbatten and Lord Brabourne at Romsey Abbey on 26th October, 1946.*

ROYAL COMMAND VARIETY. *Shaking hands with Mr. J. Arthur Rank on their arrival at the London Palladium on 4th November, 1946.*

brought up to be a representative daughter of her time, in the central tradition of normal English girlhood. The King and Queen have never encouraged her to regard herself as anything but an ordinary person, and as such she sees herself still. It is her position, not her personality, that she knows to be exceptional; and she fully understands that by showing the capacity of an ordinary woman to play an extraordinary part in the national life she best discharges the high task of royalty. Her father and grandfather before her have proved that men of normal capacity, normal tastes, and normal training are equal to the highest demands of exalted rank, provided only that they are willing to devote themselves unsparingly to public service; and it is already clear that Princess Elizabeth's direct and simple character is of a kind that fits her to walk in their footsteps. She is modest, and always willing to listen to the advice of those who have greater experience than hers. She is friendly, and capable of entering into the interests or sympathizing with the troubles of the great variety of people with whom she comes in contact. This quality, although it is innate in the sense that it proceeds from an inner kindliness of heart, has not gained expression altogether easily; for the Princess as a child had a tendency to shyness, which it has cost her a conscious effort to overcome. She has been helped by a rich fund of humour; and those who meet her for the first time, and are in many cases much shyer than she, soon discover by her easy laughter that courtly ceremonial need not be a barrier and direct and natural speech will not give offence.

Gaiety of heart and simplicity of demeanour do not prevent her being capable of great dignity, which with the passage of years will deepen into majesty when occasions of stately ceremonial demand. But it is impossible to believe that any advance of age could make Princess Elizabeth pompous. She will be saved from that by her ability in any circumstances to smile at herself.

She is a hard worker, and possesses considerable powers of concentration. She hates to leave any task unfinished, or to abandon any problem until she has mastered it. She is always ready to take great trouble over small things, especially when

PRIZE-GIVING. *On 7th November, 1946, Princess Elizabeth visited Burlington School, West London, where she presented the prizes at the prize-giving ceremony. Here one of the students is receiving the intermediate certificate of the Royal Life Saving Society.*

she suspects that things which are small to her may be of great importance to humbler people. Personal problems that are put to her in her large correspondence seldom fail to awake her personal interest. A member of the A.T.S., for instance, who had suffered an injury to her back, wrote to the Princess to say how disappointed she would be that she could not stand to see the Victory Parade. Princess Elizabeth herself intervened with the authorities and saw that the girl had a place in a window overlooking the route. Again, at the Cardiff Rally of the Girl Guides, the organizers tried to spare her fatigue at the end of an exceptionally tiring day by cancelling the march past that had been arranged. It would take too long, they said; but the Princess guessed that it would not be so regarded by the Guides. "They mustn't be disappointed," she said. "If it will take too long for them to march past me, then I will walk past them." And she did.

The heiress to the throne, then, is simple, warm-hearted, hardworking, painstaking, cultivated, humorous, and above all, friendly. In all this, fortunately, she probably resembles the great majority, and all the best, of the generation who have come to maturity with her. These are the heirs of victory; these are the men and women who have to build the world anew; the Princess is born to be their leader, and she knows she can only lead them by being one of themselves. Her equipment for the vast responsibilities that await her is that which could most be desired—the fact that in all the governing lines of her character she is a typical daughter of the Britain of her time.

In wishing her on her twenty-first birthday every happiness and blessing, her fellow countrymen from pole to pole of the world-wide Commonwealth are saluting the hope of their own future. Whether the hope will be fulfilled, whether when her time comes another great reign will be added to the noble records of the Empire's history, does not depend entirely upon her. The high vocation of monarchy is not exercised in a void. There cannot be a great king or a great queen without also a great people. That has been conspicuously shown in our history by the glorious reigns of Queen Victoria, of Queen Anne, and perhaps most of all, of the first Elizabeth. Their names glow in the tapestry of time because there is interwoven with their story the achievement of the great leaders, statesmen, discoverers and poets who exalted and sustained their throne; and also the worth and prowess of the multitude of their people whose quality made great the temper of their age.

Each of these famous ladies played her part by inspiring among her subjects, high and low, the sense of a people at unity in itself. That in the last analysis is the supreme service that monarchy can render to the present age. The endless adventure of a nation's life is one to be pursued in comradeship by sovereign and people. The impulse on which social health depends flows in a closed circuit, spreading outward from sovereign to people, but returning with equal vigour from the people to uphold and strengthen the throne. It is because Burghley and Bacon, Drake and Frobisher and Raleigh, Shakespeare and Spenser, stood about Queen Elizabeth to win and proclaim her glory that her name has become illustrious; but it is because she herself was such a woman as could inspire and keep the equal devotion of these men of such diverse genius, and could at the same time be the "mere English" of which her people were so proud, that all the forces of her stirring age could work together in harmony for the national greatness and not turn to destroy one another, as they did in the next generation under a less successful monarch.

So the place that historians of the unborn centuries will assign to Elizabeth the Second in the record of the British Crown will depend not upon her alone, and not on her subjects alone, but upon the intimacy of the relation between them. It is for her to become the centre and focus of unity for all the races and creeds of her Empire; it is for them to keep alive and intensify the sense of comradeship and common dedication to great ideals of which she is to be the leader and the symbol. It is with the determination to serve her faithfully, and through her the cause of man's upward progress for which in her Dominions she will stand, that the British peoples will pray, with Garter King of Arms in Shakespeare's drama: "Heaven, from thy endless goodness, send prosperous life, long, and ever happy, to the high and mighty princess of England, Elizabeth."

Published 1947. T.447.U. Made and Printed in Great Britain by Odhams (Watford) Ltd., Watford, Herts.